RONALD REAGAN

RONALD REAGAN

A GRAPHIC BIOGRAPHY

Written by
Andrew Helfer

Art by
Steve Buccellato
and **Joe Staton**

A NOVEL GRAPHIC from HILL AND WANG

A division of FARRAR, STRAUS AND GIROUX NEW YORK

HILL AND WANG
A DIVISION OF FARRAR, STRAUS AND GIROUX
19 UNION SQUARE WEST, NEW YORK 10003

SERIOUS COMICS GNC, LLC
23 BANK STREET, NEW YORK 10014

LIBRARY OF CONGRESS CATALOGING-IN-PUBLICATION DATA
HELFER, ANDREW.
    RONALD REAGAN : A GRAPHIC BIOGRAPHY / WRITTEN BY ANDREW HELFER ;
ART BY STEVE BUCCELLATO AND JOE STATON.— 1ST ED.
    P. CM.
    ISBN-13: 978-0-8090-9507-0 (HARDCOVER : ALK. PAPER)
    ISBN-10: 0-8090-9507-6 (HARDCOVER : ALK. PAPER)
    1. REAGAN, RONALD. 2. PRESIDENTS—UNITED STATES—BIOGRAPHY. 3. REAGAN,
RONALD—PICTORIAL WORKS. 4. GRAPHIC NOVELS. I. BUCCELLATO, STEVE. II.
STATON, JOE. III. TITLE.

E877.2. H45 2006
973.927092—DC22
[B]

                                                          2006016437

WWW.FSGBOOKS.COM
WWW.SERIOUSCOMICS.COM

RONALD REAGAN

ON JUNE 5, 2004, RONALD REAGAN, THE 40TH PRESIDENT OF THE UNITED STATES, DIED AT AGE 93.

AT THE TIME OF HIS DEATH, HE WAS SURROUNDED BY HIS WIFE, NANCY; HIS SON RON JR.; AND HIS DAUGHTER PATTI DAVIS.

SPEAKING LATER, PATTI RECALLED THE LAST MOMENTS OF THE PRESIDENT'S LIFE.

COUNTDOWN
PATTI DAVIS
MSNBC
LIVE

HE OPENED HIS EYES AND LOOKED STRAIGHT AT MY MOTHER. EYES THAT HADN'T OPENED FOR DAYS, DID. THEY WERE CLEAR, AND BLUE...AND FULL OF LOVE.

AT THAT MOMENT, NANCY HAS SAID, HER HUSBAND SEEMED SUDDENLY LUCID, AND MADE EYE CONTACT WITH HIS WIFE OF 52 YEARS FOR AN INSTANT BEFORE PASSING AWAY.

MICHAEL REAGAN, THE SON HE ADOPTED WITH HIS FIRST WIFE, THE ACTRESS JANE WYMAN, PUT IT THIS WAY:

HIS LAST EARTHLY LOOK IS AT HIS WIFE, HIS NEXT LOOK IS AT THE FACE OF GOD.

WHILE THE IMMEDIATE CAUSE OF RONALD REAGAN'S DEATH WAS PNEUMONIA, HIS DEMISE WAS ALSO THE CONCLUSION OF A LONG STRUGGLE WITH ALZHEIMER'S DISEASE, A FORM OF DEMENTIA THAT SLOWLY REDUCES THE BRAIN'S ABILITY TO CONTROL MEMORY, LANGUAGE, AND EVENTUALLY THOUGHT.

IN HIS FINAL ADDRESS TO AMERICA 10 YEARS EARLIER, REAGAN REVEALED THAT HE HAD THE DEGENERATIVE DISEASE AND EXITED PUBLIC LIFE WITH THE SAME CAREFULLY ENGINEERED MIXTURE OF DRAMA AND HUMILITY THAT HAD MARKED HIS DECADES IN THE PUBLIC EYE.

RONALD REAGAN

Nov. 5, 1994

WITH FEW EXCEPTIONS, THE MEDIA RESPECTED REAGAN'S WISH FOR PRIVACY. FOR ALMOST A DECADE, THE REAGAN FAMILY, ONCE AMERICA'S FIRST, WAS KEPT OUT OF THE SPOTLIGHT.

90 6.7 [•••] -2.1.1.1.2.1 +

SOME MAINTAINED THAT THE FORMER PRESIDENT DID NOT WANT TO BURDEN AMERICA WITH THE SIGHT OF HIS SAD, SLOW DECLINE.

OTHERS CLAIMED THAT REAGAN, HAVING SPENT DECADES PERFECTING THE ROLE, NEEDED TO BE REMEMBERED AS THE COUNTRY'S VIGOROUS, CHARISMATIC LEADER.

BOTH WERE RIGHT. FOR, IN THE END, THE IMAGE OF RONALD REAGAN WAS AS IMPORTANT AS THE MAN.

IN THE END, THE TWO BECAME INSEPARABLE.

FROM THE CIVIC-MINDED CORPORATE TELEVISION PITCHMAN...
...TO THE REPUBLICAN TORCHBEARER WITH THE SOLUTION TO AN AILING COUNTRY'S ILLS.
GOLDWATER 64 MILLER
GOLDWATER
FROM GOVERNOR OF THE STATE OF CALIFORNIA...
Biltmore
...TO THE 40TH PRESIDENT OF THE UNITED STATES.
HOLY BIBLE

BUT OF ALL THE ROLES RONALD REAGAN PLAYED, PERHAPS THE MOST IMPRESSIVE WAS HIS LAST.

AFTER A DECADE OF SECLUSION, HE REEMERGED AS A BELOVED, MOURNED, AND MISSED GIANT OF AMERICAN POLITICS AND HISTORY.

IN THE WORDS OF PRESIDENT GEORGE W. BUSH, ECHOING WHAT HAD ONCE BEEN SAID OF LINCOLN: "REAGAN BELONGS TO THE AGES NOW."

AND AS RONALD REAGAN MADE HIS FINAL EXIT, THE MYTHMAKING MACHINERY WENT INTO OVERDRIVE.

NOT ONLY WERE FLAGS HUNG AT HALF-MAST, MOMENTS OF SILENCE OBSERVED, AND A FORMAL PERIOD OF MOURNING DECLARED, BUT 100,000 PEOPLE FLOCKED TO WASHINGTON, D.C., TO PAY THEIR FINAL RESPECTS.

AFTER NUMEROUS TELEVISION RETROSPECTIVES OF REAGAN'S LIFE AND ACCOMPLISHMENTS, A LAVISH MEMORIAL SERVICE WAS HELD IN WASHINGTON, D.C.'S NATIONAL CATHEDRAL...

...FOLLOWED BY A TASTEFUL INTERMENT SERVICE OUTSIDE THE REAGAN LIBRARY IN SIMI VALLEY, CALIFORNIA.

8

RONALD REAGAN WAS THE OLDEST MAN EVER TO BE INAUGURATED PRESIDENT, AND AT THE TIME OF HIS DEATH NO U.S. PRESIDENT HAD LIVED AS LONG.

BUT WHEN REAGAN'S DEATH CAME, THE MEDIA PRESENTED THE LOSS AS A NATIONAL TRAGEDY-- AN EVENT SO WEIGHTY IT MERITED NEARLY A WEEK OF CONSTANT COVERAGE...

NOT SINCE THE TERRORIST ATTACKS OF SEPTEMBER 11, 2001, JUST THREE YEARS EARLIER, HAD THE NATION BEEN SO RIVETED BY A SINGLE NEWS STORY.

BUT THEN, AMERICA HAD NEVER SEEN A PRESIDENT LIKE RONALD REAGAN.

ALL PRESIDENTS COMMAND RESPECT-- IT COMES WITH THE POWER OF THE OFFICE.

BUT RONALD REAGAN WAS, BY TRAINING AND INCLINATION, AN ACTOR-- AND AN ACTOR IN THE ROLE OF A LIFETIME CAN WRING MORE THAN RESPECT OUT OF HIS AUDIENCE.

IN REAGAN'S TWENTY YEARS PERFORMING IN HOLLYWOOD MOTION PICTURES, HE PLAYED A "BAD GUY" ONLY ONCE.

PRODUCERS, DIRECTORS, AND FANS KNEW IMMEDIATELY THAT REAGAN WAS A MASTER AT ELICITING EMPATHY-- AND ITS COUSIN, LOVE.

RONALD REAGAN, THE SECOND SON OF NELLE AND JACK REAGAN, WAS BORN ON FEBRUARY 6, 1911, IN TAMPICO, ILLINOIS.

FATHER JACK NICKNAMED THE NEWBORN RONALD "DUTCH" BECAUSE HE LOOKED LIKE "A FAT LITTLE DUTCHMAN."

RONALD'S MOTHER AND FATHER WERE DISSIMILAR IN MANY WAYS. NELLE WAS A DEVOUT MEMBER OF THE PROTESTANT DISCIPLES OF CHRIST CHURCH. JACK WAS A NONPRACTICING CATHOLIC.

NELLE WAS HAPPILY DOMESTIC, DIVIDING HER DAYS BETWEEN HER CHILDREN AND SEWING. JACK, A SOMETIMES-TRAVELING SHOE SALESMAN, WAS SELDOM HOME.

IN HER SPARE HOURS, NELLE PRACTICED HER SINGING AND ACTING TALENTS WITH A CHURCH GROUP. IN HIS SPARE HOURS, JACK DRANK.

JACK'S DRINKING MAY HAVE HAD SOMETHING TO DO WITH HIS LACK OF SUCCESS AS A SHOE SALESMAN. OR VICE VERSA.

WHATEVER THE CAUSE, AS THE FAMILY'S FINANCIAL TROUBLES DEEPENED, THE REAGANS MOVED TO EVER CHEAPER HOMES UNTIL, IN 1920, THEY SETTLED IN THE TOWN OF DIXON, ILLINOIS.

WHILE NELLE SHIELDED HER YOUNGER SON FROM THE FAMILY'S FINANCIAL HARDSHIPS, RONALD'S BROTHER, NEIL, A MERE TWO AND A HALF YEARS OLDER, WAS EXPOSED TO THEIR HARSH REALITIES.

THE TWO SONS GREW TO REFLECT THEIR PARENTS' DISPARATE PERSONALITIES. LIKE HIS FATHER, NEIL WAS OUTGOING AND POPULAR; RONALD ECHOED HIS MOTHER'S THOUGHTFUL, BOOKISH DEMEANOR.

NEIL, TALL AND HUSKY, EXCELLED IN SPORTS AND WAS LIKED BY HIS PEERS; RONALD, SMALL AND NEARSIGHTED, PREFERRED HIS MOTHER'S COMPANIONSHIP.

AND IT WAS RONALD'S MOTHER WHO INTRODUCED HIM TO THE WORLD OF ACTING.

WITH NELLE'S ENCOURAGEMENT, RONALD JOINED HER CHURCH THEATER GROUP AND WAS SOON ENTERTAINING DIXON HOSPITAL PATIENTS.

BUT YOUNG RONALD'S FUTURE COURSE WAS HEAVILY INFLUENCED BY HIS FATHER AS WELL.

ALTHOUGH BOTH CHILDREN KNEW THEIR FATHER WAS A DRINKER, AN INCIDENT WHEN RONALD WAS ONLY 11 BROUGHT THE CONSEQUENCES OF HIS FATHER'S ALCOHOLISM INTO HARSH FOCUS.

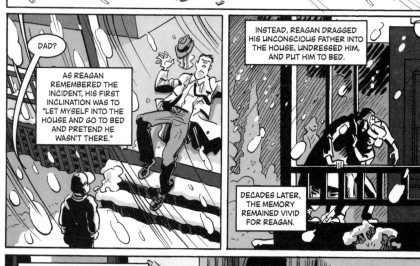

DAD?

AS REAGAN REMEMBERED THE INCIDENT, HIS FIRST INCLINATION WAS TO "LET MYSELF INTO THE HOUSE AND GO TO BED AND PRETEND HE WASN'T THERE."

INSTEAD, REAGAN DRAGGED HIS UNCONSCIOUS FATHER INTO THE HOUSE, UNDRESSED HIM, AND PUT HIM TO BED.

DECADES LATER, THE MEMORY REMAINED VIVID FOR REAGAN.

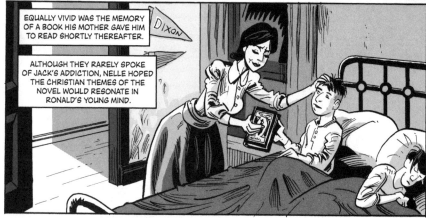

EQUALLY VIVID WAS THE MEMORY OF A BOOK HIS MOTHER GAVE HIM TO READ SHORTLY THEREAFTER.

ALTHOUGH THEY RARELY SPOKE OF JACK'S ADDICTION, NELLE HOPED THE CHRISTIAN THEMES OF THE NOVEL WOULD RESONATE IN RONALD'S YOUNG MIND.

AND RESONATE THEY DID. *THAT PRINTER OF UDELL'S* OPENS WITH A SCENE THE YOUNG REAGAN MUST HAVE FOUND DISCONCERTINGLY FAMILIAR.

A DRUNKEN FATHER; A MOTHER STARVING IN THE DEAD OF WINTER; A YOUNG SON WITHOUT HOPE.

SIXTEEN YEARS LATER, THE NOW ORPHANED SON, DICK, COMES TO A MIDWESTERN TOWN. NOT PART OF ANY CHURCH, YET CONVINCED THAT "CHRISTIANS WON'T LET ME STARVE," HE SEARCHES FOR A JOB.

GEORGE UDELL, A LOCAL PRINTER, GIVES HIM ONE.

THANKS IN PART TO HIS CHEERFUL, OPTIMISTIC ATTITUDE, DICK QUICKLY FINDS ACCEPTANCE AND BECOMES A PILLAR OF THE LOCAL CHURCHGOING COMMUNITY.

HIS PUBLIC-SPEAKING SKILLS, COUPLED WITH AN UNCANNY ABILITY TO SOLVE THE TOWN'S MORAL PROBLEMS, WIN HIM THE CONGREGATION'S LOVE AND ADMIRATION.

BY THE END OF THE NOVEL, DICK FORMALLY PROFESSES HIS FAITH IN CHRIST AND DECIDES TO DEVOTE HIS LIFE TO DOING THE MOST GOOD FOR THE MOST PEOPLE-- IN WASHINGTON, D.C.

WHEN HE WAS 66, REAGAN WOULD SAY THE BOOK "LEFT AN ABIDING BELIEF IN THE TRIUMPH OF GOOD OVER EVIL." IT ALSO SEEMED TO SERVE AS A ROAD MAP FOR HIS CAREER.

WHEN REAGAN FINISHED READING *UDELL'S*, HE TOLD HIS MOTHER HE WANTED TO BE BAPTIZED AND JOIN HER CHURCH, THE DISCIPLES OF CHRIST.

HE HAD DECIDED THAT WHEN IT CAME TO RELIGION HE WANTED MORE THAN A CHOICE BETWEEN HIS MOTHER'S OR FATHER'S "SIDE."

HE WAS DETERMINED TO BE ON THE SIDE OF THE ANGELS.

WHEN NOT ATTENDING SCHOOL, RONALD WORKED TO RAISE MONEY FOR HIS FINANCIALLY FALTERING FAMILY.

IN HIGH SCHOOL, REAGAN DISCOVERED THAT HIS THIN, WIRY BUILD WAS PERFECTLY SUITED FOR SWIMMING.

HE EXCELLED ON THE SWIM TEAM, THE ONE SPORT WHERE POOR EYESIGHT WAS NOT A HINDRANCE.

IN 1926, HIS SWIMMING TALENT ALSO QUALIFIED REAGAN FOR A JOB THAT WOULD PUT HIM IN THE PUBLIC EYE FOR THE VERY FIRST TIME.

AFTER TAKING LESSONS AT THE LOCAL YMCA, REAGAN BEGAN WORKING SUMMERS AS THE LIFEGUARD AT LOWELL PARK BEACH.

PAID $15 A WEEK, HE WOULD HOLD THE JOB TILL HE LEFT DIXON.

ALTHOUGH THERE WAS SOME QUESTION ABOUT HOW THE NEARSIGHTED REAGAN COULD SPOT FAR-OFF SWIMMERS IN TROUBLE, BY 1928 HIS EFFORTS RECEIVED PUBLIC ACCLAIM...

...IN THE FORM OF A FRONT-PAGE STORY IN THE LOCAL NEWSPAPER CELEBRATING HIS 51ST SUCCESSFUL RESCUE.

Evening Telegraph

AUGUST 3, 1928

PULLED FROM THE JAWS OF DEATH!

In another daring rescue at Lowel Park Beach, Eighteen-Year-Old lifeguard and Dixon native, Ronald Reagan Elah blaeah Swimming is fun!

YEARS LATER, REAGAN ACKNOWLEDGED THAT MANY OF THE SWIMMERS HAD DENIED THAT THEY NEEDED HELP.

FOR HIS PART, HOWEVER, REAGAN ALWAYS REMEMBERED PROUDLY THIS FIRST BRUSH WITH FAME.

IN THE FALL OF 1928, REAGAN FOLLOWED HIS GIRLFRIEND (WHO WAS ALSO HIS MINISTER'S DAUGHTER), MARGARET CLEARY, TO EUREKA COLLEGE.

LOCATED 120 MILES FROM DIXON, EUREKA WAS FOUNDED AND PRECARIOUSLY FUNDED BY THE DISCIPLES OF CHRIST CHURCH.

EUREKA COLLEGE

THE COLLEGE'S FINANCIAL TROUBLES CAME TO A HEAD SHORTLY AFTER REAGAN'S ARRIVAL, WHEN THE PRESIDENT OF EUREKA ANNOUNCED A COST-CUTTING PLAN REQUIRING THE ELIMINATION OF CERTAIN CLASSES.

WITHOUT THESE CLASSES, REAGAN LATER RECALLED, MANY STUDENTS WOULD BE UNABLE TO FULFILL THEIR DEGREE REQUIREMENTS. THEY WERE OUTRAGED.

THE STUDENTS THREATENED TO STRIKE, AND AS REAGAN TOLD THE STORY, HE WAS DRAFTED TO CONVEY THEIR REASONS AND RESOLVE.

WHAT REAGAN SAID, HE COULDN'T RECALL. WHAT HE REMEMBERED WAS THE IMPACT OF THE SPEECH ON HIS LISTENERS.

"I DISCOVERED THAT NIGHT THAT AN AUDIENCE HAD A FEEL TO IT," REAGAN SAID, "AND, IN THE PARLANCE OF THE THEATER, THAT AUDIENCE AND I WERE TOGETHER."

BY THE TIME HE WAS FINISHED, AS HE RECALLED IT, THE STUDENTS "CAME TO THEIR FEET WITH A ROAR" OF APPROVAL.

IN HIS AUTOBIOGRAPHY, REAGAN STATES THAT HIS SPEECH LAUNCHED THE STRIKE THAT EVENTUALLY SECURED THE STUDENTS' DEMANDS.

CLASSES CANCELED

212

NO CLASS

HOME ECONOMICS

EUREKA COLLEGE RECORDED NO SUCH CHAIN OF EVENTS.

BUT FOR RONALD REAGAN, THE SPEECH-- NOT ITS CONSEQUENCES-- WAS OF PRIMARY IMPORTANCE; IT PUT HIM IN FRONT OF A CROWD OF LISTENERS...

...WHOSE EMOTIONS HE COULD ELICIT ALMOST AS IF THEY WERE AN EXTENSION OF HIS OWN.

16

THOUGH INTEREST IN THE STRIKE ABATED, REAGAN WAS LEFT WITH A CLEAR DIRECTION FOR HIS FUTURE SCHOOL ACTIVITIES.

HE JOINED ALPHA EPSILON SIGMA, THE STUDENT DRAMATIC SOCIETY, EVENTUALLY WINNING AWARDS FOR HIS PERFORMANCES.

PERHAPS WITH AN EYE TOWARD ACCEPTANCE ON ANOTHER STAGE, REAGAN TRIED HIS HAND AT FOOTBALL.

HE WAS FOUND ENTHUSIASTIC BUT WANTING.

JOURNALISM PROVIDED REAGAN WITH YET ANOTHER OPPORTUNITY TO SEEK AN AUDIENCE.

REPORTING ON FOOTBALL GAMES WITNESSED FROM THE SIDELINES NEATLY SUBSTITUTED FOR HEROIC ATHLETIC EXPERIENCES ON THE FIELD.

BY JUNE 1932, AS REAGAN PREPARED TO GRADUATE FROM COLLEGE, TWO THINGS WERE CERTAIN: HE WANTED TO EARN HIS LIVING IN SHOW BUSINESS...

...AND THE DEPRESSION WAS MAKING LIFE MORE DIFFICULT THAN EVER FOR HIS FAMILY BACK HOME.

17

REAGAN'S FATHER HAD LOST HIS JOB SELLING SHOES AND HAD NO PROSPECTS FOR NEW EMPLOYMENT.

REAGAN HIMSELF HAD LITTLE ALTERNATIVE BUT TO RETURN TO HIS SUMMER LIFEGUARD POST, FOR WHICH HE WAS NOW PAID $20 A WEEK.

A JOB THAT HAD CAPTURED THE IMAGINATION OF A TEENAGER HELD LITTLE INTEREST FOR AN AMBITIOUS COLLEGE GRADUATE.

REAGAN EXPRESSED A DESIRE TO BREAK INTO RADIO TO SID ALTSCHULER, A KANSAS CITY BUSINESSMAN WHO BROUGHT HIS FAMILY TO LOWELL PARK FOR SUMMER VACATIONS.

ALTSCHULER'S ADVICE TO REAGAN WAS SIMPLE AND DIRECT.

TELL ANYONE WHO WILL LISTEN THAT YOU BELIEVE YOU HAVE A FUTURE IN THE BUSINESS, AND YOU'LL TAKE ANY KIND OF JOB, EVEN SWEEPING FLOORS, JUST TO GET IN.

IN DEPRESSION-ERA AMERICA, THAT APPROACH MADE AS MUCH SENSE AS ANY TO REAGAN.

HOPING HE COULD LAND A JOB AND SEND SOME MONEY TO HIS STRUGGLING FAMILY, REAGAN BORROWED HIS FATHER'S CAR AND DROVE OFF IN SEARCH OF OPPORTUNITY.

REAGA

HE FOUND IT AT WOC, A SMALL RADIO STATION OUTSIDE DAVENPORT, IOWA. REAGAN'S KNOWLEDGE OF FOOTBALL, COMBINED WITH HIS SELF-ASSURED PATTER, SOON MADE HIM WOC'S NUMBER-TWO ANNOUNCER OF LOCAL FOOTBALL GAMES.

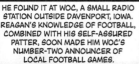

WITH THE ELECTION OF DEMOCRAT FRANKLIN DELANO ROOSEVELT TO THE PRESIDENCY AND THE BEGINNING OF NATIONWIDE NEW DEAL SOCIAL SUPPORT PROGRAMS, THINGS HAD TAKEN A POSITIVE TURN FOR REAGAN'S FATHER AS WELL. A STAUNCH ROOSEVELT SUPPORTER, HE SECURED A POSITION DISTRIBUTING PUBLIC ASSISTANCE FUNDS.

FARM CREDIT RELIEF

THROUGHOUT THE DEPRESSION, REAGAN'S FATHER AND BROTHER WOULD BOTH HAVE JOBS WITH GOVERNMENT RELIEF AGENCIES.

BUT WHILE THE STAUNCHLY DEMOCRATIC REAGAN FAMILY WEATHERED THE DEPRESSION'S DARKEST DAYS, THE REST OF AMERICA WAS NOT AS FORTUNATE.

IN THE FACE OF DECLINING REVENUES, WOC WAS FORCED TO MERGE WITH A LARGER STATION, WHO.

ALTHOUGH REAGAN'S POSITION CHANGED, IT WAS FOR THE BETTER. AT THE NEWLY CONSOLIDATED STATION, HE WOULD PROVIDE PLAY-BY-PLAY REPORTING OF CHICAGO CUBS BASEBALL GAMES.

NOT, HOWEVER, FROM THE STADIUM, BUT FROM THE WHO STATION IN DES MOINES, IOWA!

POP CORN

WHO

RATHER THAN BLANDLY READ PLAYS AS THEY CAME OFF THE TELETYPE, RADIO ANNOUNCERS TRIED TO INJECT A "YOU ARE THERE" IMMEDIACY TO THEIR REPORTS.

AT THIS, REAGAN EXCELLED. HE SAW IT AS AN OPPORTUNITY TO HONE HIS TALENTS AS A PUBLIC SPEAKER, AND HIS ACCOUNTS MADE LISTENERS BELIEVE HE WAS AN EYEWITNESS TO THE GAMES.

REAGAN LOVED TO TELL THE STORY OF THE TIME THE NEWSWIRE BROKE DOWN, LEAVING HIM WITHOUT THE FACTS THAT SERVED AS THE BARE-BONES BASIS FOR HIS REPORT.

STALLING FOR TIME, REAGAN SUMMONED UP ALL HIS STORYTELLING SKILLS TO "REPORT" A SERIES OF FOUL TIPS FROM THE BATTER, ALL OF WHICH LANDED JUST SHY OF FAIR TERRITORY.

WHEN THE WIRE RETURNED TO LIFE 20 MINUTES LATER, HOWEVER, REAGAN LEARNED THE BATTER HAD POPPED OUT WITH THE VERY FIRST PITCH.

TWENTY MINUTES AGO, DUTCH.

AUDIENCES, REAGAN KNEW, TUNED IN TO HEAR A GOOD STORY WELL TOLD.

SOMETIMES THE FACTS ONLY GOT IN THE WAY.

AS HIS SPORTSCASTING REPUTATION GREW, REAGAN DECIDED IT WAS TIME FOR HIM TO TRY TO EXPAND HIS AUDIENCE.

WHEN, IN 1937, THE STATION SENT HIM TO SEE THE *CHICAGO CUBS* SPRING TRAINING IN CALIFORNIA, REAGAN MADE A SIDE TRIP TO HOLLYWOOD.

THERE HE MET UP WITH JOY HODGES, A FORMER RADIO COWORKER WHO HAD BECOME A SUCCESSFUL HOLLYWOOD SINGER.

LOSE THE GLASSES...

...TURNED OUT TO BE THE BEST ADVICE SHE COULD HAVE GIVEN THE ASPIRING ACTOR.

HODGES INTRODUCED REAGAN, NOW SANS EYEWEAR, TO GEORGE WARD, HER HOLLYWOOD AGENT.

HMMM...CLEAN-CUT, FRIENDLY LOOKING. I BET YOU'RE JUST THE TYPE WARNER BROS. IS LOOKING FOR.

I'M GONNA DO US BOTH A FAVOR AND CALL JACK WARNER ABOUT YOU RIGHT NOW.

REAGAN TOOK A SCREEN TEST AND RETURNED HOME.

WHEN WARNERS QUICKLY OFFERED HIM A CONTRACT AT $200 A WEEK, THE AGENT ASKED REAGAN WHAT HE WANTED HIM TO DO.

SIGN IT BEFORE THEY CHANGE THEIR MINDS!

WITH THE SELF-DEPRECATING GOOD HUMOR IN THE MIDST OF LIFE-ALTERING EVENTS THAT WOULD BE HIS TRADEMARK, REAGAN SEALED THE DEAL.

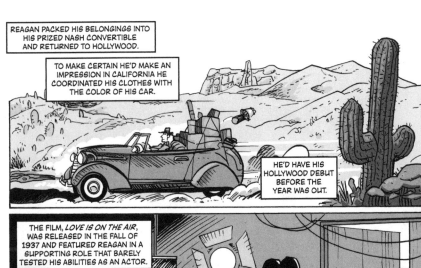

REAGAN PACKED HIS BELONGINGS INTO HIS PRIZED NASH CONVERTIBLE AND RETURNED TO HOLLYWOOD.

TO MAKE CERTAIN HE'D MAKE AN IMPRESSION IN CALIFORNIA HE COORDINATED HIS CLOTHES WITH THE COLOR OF HIS CAR.

HE'D HAVE HIS HOLLYWOOD DEBUT BEFORE THE YEAR WAS OUT.

THE FILM, *LOVE IS ON THE AIR*, WAS RELEASED IN THE FALL OF 1937 AND FEATURED REAGAN IN A SUPPORTING ROLE THAT BARELY TESTED HIS ABILITIES AS AN ACTOR.

IN IT, HE PLAYED THE PART OF A RADIO ANNOUNCER.

HIS NEXT FILM, *HOLLYWOOD HOTEL*, WAS NOTABLE NOT FOR HIS ON-SCREEN PERFORMANCE BUT RATHER FOR THE SOCIAL CONTACTS HE MADE ON THE SET.

THE FILM'S CONCEPT CAME FROM LOUELLA PARSONS, THE POWERFUL HOLLYWOOD GOSSIP COLUMNIST. AS IT HAPPENED, PARSONS HAD ALSO BEEN RAISED IN DIXON.

PARSONS, WHOSE WHISPERS COULD MAKE OR BREAK HOLLYWOOD CAREERS, IMMEDIATELY LIKED THE YOUNG FELLOW DIXONITE.

POSITIVE PRESS WOULD FOLLOW, BUT FIRST PARSONS DECIDED TO PLAY MATCHMAKER WITH TWO OF HER FAVORITE YOUNG STARS.

STARLETS

STAR

REAGAN MET ACTRESS JANE WYMAN ON THE SET OF THE 1938 FILM *BROTHER RAT*. THE NOT-QUITE-DIVORCED WYMAN IMMEDIATELY PURSUED REAGAN...

...BUT THE APPEARANCE OF IMPROPRIETY THAT A SEMI-ILLICIT RELATIONSHIP MIGHT CREATE CAUSED REAGAN TO HESITATE.

BUT PARSONS, WRITING IN HER NEWSPAPER COLUMN ABOUT THE TWO CHARMING YOUNG "STARS OF TOMORROW," CLEARED THE WAY FOR PUBLIC ACCEPTANCE...

...AND THEIR JANUARY 1940 STORYBOOK WEDDING.

THEN, AFTER JUST TWO YEARS OF APPEARING IN B MOVIES, REAGAN MADE THE LEAP TO THE NEXT LEVEL.

HE LANDED THE PIVOTAL SUPPORTING ROLE OF FOOTBALL LEGEND GEORGE GIPP IN *KNUTE ROCKNE ALL AMERICAN*.

THOUGH GIPP DIES EARLY IN THE FILM, HIS MEMORY INSPIRES COACH ROCKNE AND GIPP'S NOTRE DAME TEAMMATES TO VICTORY.

DECADES LATER, THE FILM'S STIRRING CALL TO ACTION, "GO OUT AND WIN ONE FOR THE GIPPER," WOULD INSPIRE THE SUPPORTERS OF NOT REAGAN THE ACTOR, BUT REAGAN THE POLITICIAN...

...SO SEAMLESSLY DID THE ROLES BLUR TOGETHER.

1941 WAS A GOOD YEAR FOR THE REAGANS, DESPITE THE DEATH OF RONALD'S FATHER. IN JANUARY WYMAN GAVE BIRTH TO DAUGHTER MAUREEN...

...AND, LATER, REAGAN BEGAN WORK ON HIS MOST FAMOUS FILM, *KINGS ROW*.

IN IT, REAGAN PLAYED A CHARACTER WHO WAS EMOTIONALLY ALMOST IDENTICAL TO HIMSELF: DRAKE McHUGH, A GOOD-HUMORED, SOCIABLE, OPTIMISTIC YOUNG MAN...

...BUT ONE WHOSE HAPPY-GO-LUCKY LIFE COMES TO AN ABRUPT HALT WHEN A SADISTIC DOCTOR UNNECESSARILY AMPUTATES HIS LEGS.

MOVIE CRITICS CONSIDERED REAGAN'S PERFORMANCE THE HIGH POINT OF HIS ACTING CAREER. REAGAN AGREED. IN 1964, McHUGH'S ANGUISHED CRY OF REALIZATION...

WHERE'S THE REST OF ME?!

...WAS USED AS THE TITLE OF REAGAN'S CAREER-REDEFINING AUTOBIOGRAPHY. THE REST OF HIM, HE THEN REVEALED, WAS MEANT FOR THE POLITICAL ARENA.

BUT TWO DECADES EARLIER, REAGAN WAS POISED FOR STARDOM WHEN, ON DECEMBER 7, 1941, JAPANESE PLANES BOMBED AMERICAN SHIPS AT PEARL HARBOR, HAWAII. THE NEXT DAY, PRESIDENT ROOSEVELT ANNOUNCED THE UNITED STATES' ENTRANCE INTO THE SECOND WORLD WAR.

U.S. ARMED FORCES
YOU'RE DRAFTED!
—Uncle Sam

AS AMERICAN TROOPS HEADED OFF TO BATTLE THE AXIS POWERS IN EUROPE AND ASIA, REAGAN WAS CALLED UP FOR ACTIVE MILITARY SERVICE.

BUT REAGAN NEVER SAW COMBAT OVERSEAS. HE NEVER EVEN LEFT CALIFORNIA.

INSTEAD, AFTER A BRIEF STINT WITH A CAVALRY UNIT IN SAN FRANCISCO, HE WAS ASSIGNED TO THE FIRST MOTION PICTURE UNIT OF THE ARMY AIR FORCE.

FORT ROACH

HEADQUARTERED IN LOS ANGELES, A STONE'S THROW FROM REAGAN'S HOME, THE MOTION PICTURE UNIT MADE TRAINING FILMS AND MOVIES TO LIFT THE MORALE OF THE GENERAL PUBLIC.

MOVIES LIKE *TARGET TOKYO*, *BEYOND THE LINE OF DUTY*, AND *THE REAR GUNNER*-- ALL EITHER NARRATED BY OR FEATURING REAGAN-- PROMOTED AMERICA'S WARTIME VALUES.

THE FILMS WERE DESIGNED TO INSTILL PATRIOTIC FEELINGS IN THEIR AUDIENCES, BUT THEY AFFECTED REAGAN AS WELL.

BY THE TIME VICTORY WAS DECLARED, REAGAN HAD SO COMPLETELY EMBRACED THE IMAGES THAT HE WOULD LATER SPEAK AS IF HE HAD BEEN A FIRSTHAND WITNESS TO THE WAR'S ATROCITIES.

WITH THE WAR OVER, REAGAN RETURNED TO CIVILIAN CINEMA... WITH ALL ITS PERKS.

EVEN BEFORE ENTERING THE MILITARY, REAGAN HAD SIGNED HOLLYWOOD'S FIRST MILLION-DOLLAR CONTRACT, NEGOTIATED BY HIS THEN-AGENT, MCA'S LEW WASSERMAN. OUT OF GRATITUDE, REAGAN WOULD SPEND MUCH OF HIS CAREER RETURNING THE FAVOR.

AND, OUTRAGED BY THE CHUNK THE GOVERNMENT TOOK FROM HIS HUGE PAYCHECK, HE BEGAN A LIFELONG MISSION: FIGHTING TAXES.

BUT DESPITE HIS HEFTY PAYCHECK, REAGAN WAS ONCE AGAIN ACTING IN B PICTURES.

HIS BIG-SCREEN STAR FADING, REAGAN TOOK SOME TIME OFF TO CONTEMPLATE FUTURE CAREER MOVES.

HE DECIDED TO FOCUS ON THE SCREEN ACTORS GUILD (SAG). HAVING SERVED ON SAG'S BOARD OF DIRECTORS SHORTLY BEFORE BEING DRAFTED, REAGAN ALREADY KNEW THE UNION.

ALTHOUGH A RANK-AND-FILE MEMBER OF THE UNION SINCE 1937, REAGAN HAD BEEN RELUCTANT TO SERVE ON ITS BOARD. THAT CHANGED WHEN HE MET HIS FELLOW BOARD MEMBERS.

"MY EDUCATION WAS COMPLETED WHEN I WALKED INTO THE BOARDROOM," REAGAN RECALLED. "I KNEW THAT I WAS BEGINNING TO FIND THE REST OF ME."

REAGAN WOULD OMIT THE FACT THAT HIS WIFE, JANE WYMAN, WAS AMONG THE "FAMOUS MEN OF THE BUSINESS" ALREADY SERVING ON THE BOARD...

...EVEN THOUGH IT HAS BEEN SAID THAT WYMAN HERSELF SUGGESTED HE BE APPOINTED TO THE BOARD WHEN A VACANCY AROSE.

BUT WHILE REAGAN WAS ONLY TOO HAPPY TO ACCEPT A SEAT ON THE SAG BOARD, THE UNION HE WAS RETURNING TO IN 1946 WAS QUITE DIFFERENT FROM THE ONE HE'D LEFT FOUR YEARS EARLIER.

SAG, A BEACON OF UNION STABILITY, WAS IN THE UNENVIABLE POSITION OF MEDIATING BETWEEN WARRING FACTIONS OF OTHER HOLLYWOOD TRADE UNIONS.

THIS INCLUDED NEGOTIATING THE SETTLEMENT OF A SERIES OF DISPUTES BETWEEN THE CONFERENCE OF STUDIO UNIONS (CSU) AND THE INTERNATIONAL ALLIANCE OF THEATRICAL STAGE EMPLOYEES (IATSE).

IT WAS DURING THESE ESPECIALLY FRUSTRATING NEGOTIATIONS THAT REAGAN FIRST CAME TO BELIEVE CERTAIN OUTSIDE FORCES WERE ATTEMPTING TO INFLUENCE THE OUTCOME OF UNION DECISIONS.

DURING THE WAR, SOVIET COMMUNISTS WERE AMERICA'S ALLIES, PARTNERS IN THE FIGHT AGAINST FASCIST GERMANY AND ITALY, AND IMPERIALIST JAPAN. BUT WHEN THE WAR ENDED, SO DID THE ALLIANCE.

IT WAS AN AWAKENING FOR REAGAN. "I WAS TRULY SO NAIVE," HE WOULD LATER RECALL. "I THOUGHT THE NEAREST COMMUNISTS WERE FIGHTING IN STALINGRAD."

VIEWED WITH SUSPICION AND FEAR BEFORE WORLD WAR II, THE COMMUNISTS EMERGED AS AMERICA'S PRINCIPAL ENEMY AT THE WAR'S CONCLUSION.

AS THE NEGOTIATIONS BETWEEN THE CSU AND IATSE FOR CONTROL OF HOLLYWOOD WORKERS GROUND TO A STANDSTILL, REAGAN INCREASINGLY VIEWED ONE MAN AS THE CAUSE OF THE PROBLEM:

HERBERT SORRELL, THE BELLIGERENT, ANTAGONISTIC PRESIDENT OF THE CSU.

UNDER SORRELL'S LEADERSHIP, THE CSU HAD OFTEN RESORTED TO INTIMIDATION AND VIOLENCE TO MEET ITS GOAL OF UNITING THE HOLLYWOOD TRADE UNIONS UNDER ITS BANNER.

UNABLE TO SEE ANY VALID REASONS FOR SORRELL'S REFUSAL TO COMPROMISE, REAGAN CONCLUDED IT WAS A CLEAR INDICATION OF COMMUNIST INFLUENCE.

IN HIS AUTOBIOGRAPHY, REAGAN DESCRIBES AN UNEXPECTED LATE-NIGHT VISIT BY MYSTERIOUS MEN FROM A "WELL-KNOWN GOVERNMENT AGENCY."

THE MEN CONFIRMED REAGAN'S SUSPICIONS: COMMUNISTS HAD INFILTRATED THE TRADE UNIONS. AND THEY WENT ONE STEP FURTHER:

REAGAN HIMSELF, THEY REVEALED, WAS NOW A TARGET OF THE COMMUNISTS.

BY THE TIME THE VISITORS LEFT, REAGAN WAS CONVINCED A COMMUNIST CONSPIRACY EXISTED, AND HE KNEW WHAT WAS AT STAKE:

"THEIR AIM WAS TO GAIN ECONOMIC CONTROL OF THE MOTION PICTURE INDUSTRY IN ORDER TO FINANCE THEIR ACTIVITIES AND SUBVERT THE SCREEN FOR THEIR PROPAGANDA," REAGAN SAID YEARS LATER.

REAGAN WAS CHARGED WITH A NEW SENSE OF PURPOSE: TO COMBAT THE COMMUNIST MENACE.

AS HE REMEMBERS IT, WHEN HE LET WARNER BROS. KNOW ABOUT THE PLOT AGAINST HIM, THE STUDIO SENT HIM DIRECTLY TO THE POLICE TO BE LICENSED TO CARRY A GUN.

AND WHEN RONALD REAGAN WAS ELECTED PRESIDENT OF THE SCREEN ACTORS GUILD THAT YEAR, HIS MISSION TRANSCENDED INDUSTRY INTERESTS. HE WAS DETERMINED...

...TO CREATE A UNION CLEAN OF ANY COMMUNIST INFLUENCE, AND TO USE THAT UNION AS A WEAPON AGAINST THE FORCES OF COMMUNISM.

IN 1947 REAGAN AND WYMAN BECAME SECRET FBI INFORMANTS, CODE-NAMED T-10 AND T-11. BOTH IDENTIFIED MEMBERS OF SAG THEY BELIEVED WERE COMMUNISTS.

AFTER MEETING IN A POSH NEW YORK CITY HOTEL, MOVIE PRODUCERS ISSUED "THE WALDORF STATEMENT," WHICH DECLARED THEIR INTENT TO FIRE "ALLEGED SUBVERSIVE AND DISLOYAL ELEMENTS IN HOLLYWOOD."

AS SAG PRESIDENT, REAGAN SUPPORTED A RESOLUTION STATING THAT "NO ONE SHALL BE ELIGIBLE FOR OFFICE... UNLESS HE SIGNS AN AFFIDAVIT STIPULATING HE IS NOT A MEMBER OF THE (COMMUNIST) PARTY."

THE STATEMENT ALSO INVITED TALENT GUILDS LIKE SAG TO ASSIST IN ROOTING OUT SUBVERSIVES WHO HAD AVOIDED EXPOSURE.

A NEW ERA IN HOLLYWOOD WAS POISED TO BEGIN: THE ERA OF THE BLACKLIST.

IN WASHINGTON, D.C., THE HOUSE UN-AMERICAN ACTIVITIES COMMITTEE (HUAC) WAS MEETING, AND ON OCTOBER 25, REAGAN TESTIFIED AS A "FRIENDLY WITNESS."

ALTHOUGH HE AVOIDED NAMING ALLEGED COMMUNISTS TO THE COMMITTEE, HE INSINUATED THAT OTHERS BELIEVED HERB SORRELL WAS A PARTY MEMBER.

REAGAN'S OUTSPOKEN LOYALTY TO MANAGEMENT THROUGH THE YEARS OF BLACKLISTING MADE HIM DISTINCTLY UNPOPULAR WITH THE LEFT-LEANING INTELLECTUALS IN ENTERTAINMENT'S UPPER ECHELONS.

THEIR ENMITY HELPED DEEPEN HIS DISDAIN FOR PEOPLE WHO HE FELT SPENT MORE TIME THINKING THAN GETTING THINGS DONE.

BY THE END OF 1947 REAGAN WAS FIRMLY ESTABLISHED AS THE PRESIDENT OF ONE OF HOLLYWOOD'S MOST POWERFUL UNIONS.

HIS LONG WORKING HOURS AND PERSONAL WAR AGAINST COMMUNISM MAY HAVE BEEN FACTORS IN THE DISSOLUTION OF HIS MARRIAGE TO WYMAN.

REGARDLESS OF THE REASONS, WYMAN WAS UNHAPPY. AS REAGAN DELIVERED AN IMPASSIONED ANTICOMMUNIST SPEECH TO A GROUP OF FRIENDS, SHE WAS HEARD TO REMARK:

I'M SO BORED WITH HIM. I'LL EITHER KILL HIM OR KILL MYSELF.

PERHAPS FOLLOWING HER HUSBAND'S LEAD, WYMAN THREW HERSELF INTO HER WORK, WINNING A BEST ACTRESS ACADEMY AWARD FOR HER ROLE AS A DEAF MUTE IN THE FILM *JOHNNY BELINDA.*

HER SUCCESS ONLY ADDED TO THE FRICTION BETWEEN THEM. AT THE ACADEMY AWARDS CEREMONY, REAGAN TOLD HEDDA HOPPER:

IF THIS COMES TO A DIVORCE, I THINK I'LL NAME JOHNNY BELINDA AS A CORESPONDENT.

BY 1948, THEIR MARRIAGE WAS OVER.

PACKING A FEW OF HIS TREASURED POSSESSIONS, REAGAN MOVED INTO AN APARTMENT IN THE SAME BUILDING HE HAD LIVED IN BEFORE HIS MARRIAGE.

AFTER A BRIEF PERIOD OF SECLUSION, REAGAN STARTED DATING AGAIN, BUT HIS EFFORTS WERE HALFHEARTED AT BEST.

IT WAS DIFFICULT FOR HIM TO ACCEPT HIS WIFE'S DECISION TO END THEIR MARRIAGE. WHILE NEITHER REAGAN NOR WYMAN EVER REVEALED THE DETAILS OF THEIR BREAKUP, JUST BEFORE THE DIVORCE, REAGAN WROTE TO A FAN CONCERNED ABOUT THE RUMORS:

Janie is still a pretty sick girl in the mind, but I'm hoping that things will be different when she gets over this nervousness... I know she loves me even though she thinks she doesn't.

LOOKING BACK, REAGAN WOULD REFER TO THE YEAR 1949 AS HIS "ANNUS HORRIBILUS."

HE WAS DATING SOME OF HOLLYWOOD'S MOST DESIRABLE YOUNG ACTRESSES, BUT USUALLY WITH UNHAPPY RESULTS.

ACTRESS DORIS DAY RECALLED THEIR DATES TOGETHER:

IT WASN'T REALLY CONVERSATION, IT WAS RATHER TALKING AT YOU...I REMEMBER TELLING HIM THAT HE SHOULD BE TOURING THE COUNTRY MAKING SPEECHES.

HERS WOULD TURN OUT TO BE PRESCIENT ADVICE.

IN LATE 1949, REAGAN'S LUCK BEGAN TO CHANGE WHEN HE RECEIVED A CALL FROM THE DIRECTOR MERVYN LeROY.

BUT REAGAN'S HOPE THAT THE FAMED DIRECTOR WAS CALLING TO OFFER HIM A PART IN A FILM WERE DASHED WHEN LeROY SAID HE NEEDED REAGAN'S ASSISTANCE WITH A SAG MATTER.

LeROY WAS CALLING ABOUT NANCY DAVIS, A YOUNG MGM CONTRACT PLAYER WHO HAD BEEN RECEIVING LEFT-WING LITERATURE IN THE MAIL AND HAD RECENTLY LEARNED HER NAME WAS INCLUDED IN COMMUNIST PARTY ROSTERS.

CONCERNED THAT THIS MISTAKEN AFFILIATION MIGHT DAMAGE HER CAREER, LeROY ASKED REAGAN TO CHECK THE GUILD FILES TO CLEAR UP THE MATTER.

DAVIS

REAGAN DID AS ASKED AND REPORTED BACK TO LeROY THAT DAVIS WAS BEING CONFUSED WITH ANOTHER WOMAN WITH THE SAME NAME.

LeROY INSISTED THAT REAGAN DELIVER THE GOOD NEWS HIMSELF BY TAKING NANCY OUT TO DINNER. IN LATER YEARS, NANCY REVEALED THAT SHE HAD PRESSURED LeROY TO CONTACT REAGAN IN THE FIRST PLACE, AS AN EXCUSE FOR THE TWO TO MEET.

THOUGH IT TOOK ALMOST THREE YEARS OF DATING, REAGAN AND DAVIS WERE MARRIED ON MARCH 4, 1952. FEWER THAN NINE MONTHS LATER, THEIR FIRST CHILD WAS BORN.

UNLIKE JANE WYMAN, DAVIS HAD LITTLE CHANCE OF OUTSHINING REAGAN WITH HER ACTING SKILLS. FROM THE START, HER CAREER TOOK A BACKSEAT TO THEIR PARTNERSHIP. IN 1950, SHE JOINED THE SAG BOARD; SHE WOULD SERVE ALONGSIDE HER HUSBAND UNTIL 1960.

IN 1952, AS HIS MOTION PICTURE CAREER CONTINUED ITS DOWNWARD SPIRAL WITH FILMS LIKE *BEDTIME FOR BONZO*, REAGAN'S DUTIES AS PRESIDENT OF SAG ASSUMED A NEW IMPORTANCE.

REAGAN'S LONGTIME AGENT AND FRIEND, LEW WASSERMAN, WANTED TO CHANGE EXISTING SAG RULES.

WASSERMAN AND HIS COMPANY, MCA, HAD DECIDED IT WAS TIME TO TAKE ADVANTAGE OF THE RISING POPULARITY OF TELEVISION BY FORMING REVUE PRODUCTIONS, WHICH WOULD BE AN MCA SUBSIDIARY.

IT WOULD PRODUCE PROGRAMS FOR TELEVISION AND USE THE ACTORS REPRESENTED BY THE MCA AGENCY.

BUT SAG RULES STOOD IN THE WAY. ACCORDING TO ITS POLICY, ACTORS WERE NOT ALLOWED TO BE REPRESENTED BY AGENTS WHO WERE ALSO MOVIE PRODUCERS.

THIS CONFLICT OF INTEREST COULD RESULT IN ACTORS BEING GIVEN A RAW DEAL BY THEIR SELF-INTERESTED AGENTS.

REAGAN HAD ALREADY INDIRECTLY BENEFITED FROM A VERSION OF THIS RULE. IN 1947, SAG PRESIDENT AND ACTOR ROBERT MONTGOMERY WAS ABOUT TO PRODUCE AS WELL AS ACT IN A FILM.

PREZ

ALTHOUGH THE GUILD GAVE MONTGOMERY A SPECIAL WAIVER TO DO BOTH, HE STILL HAD TO RESIGN HIS PRESIDENCY, ALLOWING REAGAN TO REPLACE HIM.

BUT WASSERMAN AND MCA WERE NOT LOOKING FOR CASE-BY-CASE PERMISSION; THEY WANTED A BLANKET WAIVER THAT WOULD ENABLE THEM TO COMBINE UNRESTRICTED ACCESS TO BOTH TALENT AND THE MEANS OF PRODUCTION...

...AN ARRANGEMENT THAT WOULD PROVE TO BE A GOLD MINE AS TELEVISION AUDIENCES GREW.

IN EXCHANGE FOR THIS WAIVER, MCA AGREED TO GIVE ACTORS ADDITIONAL MONIES WHEN THEIR WORK WAS REUSED...

...THUS SETTLING THE ISSUE OF RESIDUALS, LONG A SOURCE OF DISAGREEMENT BETWEEN SAG AND TELEVISION PRODUCERS CONSCIOUS OF THE VALUE OF RERUNS.

NO OTHER AGENCIES OR PRODUCERS WERE INFORMED OF THE MCA AGREEMENT; NONE WERE INVITED TO RECEIVE A SIMILAR WAIVER IF THEY AGREED TO ABIDE BY THE SAME TERMS AS MCA.

MCA'S EXCLUSIVE WAIVER WAS ONE OF HOLLYWOOD'S BEST-KEPT SECRETS AND GAVE THE FLEDGLING PRODUCTION COMPANY AN ADVANTAGE OVER ALL OTHERS.

AS WRITER GARRY WILLS POINTS OUT: "THAT ACT, MORE THAN ANYTHING ELSE REAGAN DID IN HOLLYWOOD-- AS ACTOR, AS LABOR LEADER, AS ANTICOMMUNIST-- SHAPED THE FUTURE OF HOLLYWOOD."

HOLLYWOOD INC.
AGENCY PRODUCTIONS

IT WAS RESPONSIBLE FOR PULLING POWER AWAY FROM THE STUDIOS AND PLACING IT IN THE HANDS OF THIS NEWLY CREATED "SUPERAGENT" WHO CONTROLLED-- AND PROFITED FROM-- EVERY ASPECT OF PRODUCTION.

HOWEVER HE HAD CHANGED HOLLYWOOD'S FUTURE, REAGAN'S FUTURE AS A BIG-SCREEN ACTOR LOOKED GRIM IN 1952.

IN AN ATTEMPT TO SALVAGE HIS REPUTATION, REAGAN DECIDED TO TURN DOWN ALL THE SECOND-RATE SCRIPTS HE WAS OFFERED.

GOOD SCRIPTS

BAD SCRIPTS

WHEN THE DUST CLEARED, THERE WAS PRECIOUS LITTLE LEFT TO CHOOSE FROM.

ACCORDING TO REAGAN, HE "WENT 14 MONTHS AND TURNED DOWN HALF A MILLION DOLLARS' WORTH OF FILMS."

MCA CAME TO THE RESCUE, THIS TIME THROUGH VICE PRESIDENT TAFT SCHREIBER.

SCHREIBER SUGGESTED REAGAN HEAD OUT TO THE DESERT... TO LAS VEGAS, TO BE PRECISE.

GOOD SCRIPTS

BAD SCRIPTS

WELCOME TO LAS VEGAS

LAST FRONTIER VILLAGE

THERE REAGAN WOULD PERFORM FOR TWO WEEKS AS THE MASTER OF CEREMONIES FOR A VARIETY SHOW AT THE APTLY NAMED "LAST FRONTIER" CASINO-HOTEL.

SILVER SLIPPER GAMBLING HALL BINGO

REAGAN LATER CLAIMED THE ONLY REASON HE GAVE IT A WHIRL WAS BECAUSE HIS HOROSCOPE TOLD HIM TO.

NEVERTHELESS, REAGAN HAD FOND MEMORIES OF HIS TWO WEEKS ON THE VEGAS NIGHTCLUB CIRCUIT. BUT IT WASN'T BECAUSE OF ANY STRENUOUS ACTING.

BEYOND SIMPLY INTRODUCING A NUMBER OF ACTS, HE APPEARED WITH A MALE QUARTET CALLED THE CONTINENTALS THAT SANG AND DID LIGHT COMEDY ROUTINES.

REAGAN HIMSELF CALLED THE CONTINENTALS' WORK "HOKEY, BUT VERY FUNNY."

HIS PART IN THE ACT, HE RECALLED, WAS TO APPEAR AS "A REAL SONG AND DANCE MAN" WHO NEVER GETS THE CHANCE TO DO EITHER.

WHEN IT WAS ANNOUNCED I WAS GOING TO DO A FLOOR SHOW, SOMEONE ASKED, "WHAT'S HE GOING TO DO?" THAT'S A VERY GOOD QUESTION. I WISH I HAD A GOOD ANSWER. SO DOES THE FELLOW WHO ASKED ME...HE RUNS THIS PLACE!

NO FANCY SCRIPT WAS NECESSARY, NO CRITIC'S OPINION MATTERED. APPEARING LIVE, REAGAN HAD THE AUDIENCE IN THE PALM OF HIS HAND.

REAGAN WAS SHOWERED WITH OFFERS FROM HOTELS ACROSS THE COUNTRY. HE TURNED THEM ALL DOWN.

MCA WAS PREPARING A MUCH LARGER AUDIENCE FOR HIM.

WELCOME TO LAS VEGAS

BACK IN LOS ANGELES, MCA'S SCHREIBER PROPOSED A WEEKLY DRAMATIC TELEVISION SERIES TO DEBUT IN 1954, WITH REAGAN STARRING IN SIX EPISODES WHILE SERVING AS HOST TO INTRODUCE THE OTHERS.

MCA'S REVUE TELEVISION PRODUCTION ARM WOULD PACKAGE THE SHOW AND SELL IT TO AN ADVERTISING AGENCY, WHO IN TURN WOULD SELL IT TO GENERAL ELECTRIC, THE SHOW'S SPONSOR.

THE ICING ON THE CAKE: MCA WOULD COLLECT A 10% AGENT'S FEE FROM SALARIES PAID TO REAGAN AND ALL OTHER ACTORS ON THE SHOW.

THIS ARRANGEMENT WAS POSSIBLE DUE TO THE WAIVER REAGAN AND SAG HAD GIVEN TO MCA IN 1952.

REVUE

BATTON, BARTON DURSTINE & OSBORN

REAGAN WAS HAPPY TO ACCEPT THEIR OFFER. AS REAGAN HIMSELF WOULD STATE, ONCE AGAIN MCA WAS "THE CAVALRY TO THE RESCUE."

BUT SERVING AS THE HOST OF REVUE PRODUCTIONS' *GENERAL ELECTRIC THEATER* WOULD ULTIMATELY MEAN MUCH MORE THAN A GENEROUS PAYCHECK.

THE NEW JOB'S GREATEST BENEFIT STEMMED FROM REAGAN'S ANCILLARY DUTIES FOR GENERAL ELECTRIC.

©CBS

ACCORDING TO REAGAN, IT WAS MCA'S IDEA TO "HANG THE PACKAGE ON SOME PERSONAL APPEARANCE TOURS."

FOR REAGAN, THIS SEALED THE DEAL. PERHAPS HE WAS THINKING OF WHAT PRESIDENT EISENHOWER'S SECRETARY OF DEFENSE HAD RECENTLY SAID: "WHAT'S GOOD FOR THE COUNTRY IS GOOD FOR GENERAL MOTORS AND VICE VERSA."

THE SAME WOULD APPPLY TO GENERAL ELECTRIC.

AS *GENERAL ELECTRIC THEATER* HIT THE AIRWAVES, REAGAN HIT THE ROAD, TRAVELING BY TRAIN (HE HAD A FEAR OF FLYING THAT WOULD LAST UNTIL HIS POLITICAL CAREER TOOK OFF) TO THE FIRST OF THE 135 GE PLANTS HE'D VISIT OVER THE NEXT EIGHT YEARS.

INITIALLY, REAGAN DID LITTLE MORE THAN MEET AND GREET GE EMPLOYEES.

HE GAVE NO SPEECHES BECAUSE THE GE PUBLIC RELATIONS MAN ASSIGNED TO REAGAN DIDN'T WANT TO WRITE THEM.

BUT WHEN REAGAN VOLUNTEERED TO DO IT HIMSELF, THE AUDIENCES' RESPONSES IMPRESSED THE GE BRASS.

AS HE TRAVELED AROUND THE COUNTRY, SOMETIMES FOR WEEKS WITHOUT A BREAK, REAGAN SPOKE TO THOUSANDS OF PEOPLE ABOUT HIS VISION FOR AMERICA.

CITY OF ANNENDALE CHAMBER OF COMMERCE

AS REAGAN TOURED THE COUNTRY *GENERAL ELECTRIC THEATER* BECAME A HIT TELEVISION SERIES.

DURING THE 1956-57 SEASON ONLY *THE ED SULLIVAN SHOW* AND *I LOVE LUCY* HAD HIGHER RATINGS.

THE SHOW HELD A HIDDEN BENEFIT FOR REAGAN-- IT INTRODUCED HIM TO A GENERATION OF VIEWERS THAT HAD NEVER SEEN A RONALD REAGAN FILM.

TO THE FIRST TELEVISION GENERATION, RONALD REAGAN WAS A TV STAR.

BUT AFTER PEAKING IN 1957, *GENERAL ELECTRIC THEATER* BEGAN A SLOW DECLINE. IN SEPTEMBER 1961, NBC PLACED *BONANZA* AGAINST *GE THEATER* IN THE 9 P.M. SUNDAY TIME SLOT.

THE FULL-COLOR WESTERN BEAT OUT THE BLACK-AND-WHITE ANTHOLOGY SERIES. IN SEPTEMBER 1962, *GENERAL ELECTRIC THEATER* WAS CANCELED.

GIVEN 24 HOURS' NOTICE BY GE, REAGAN WAS LET GO.

REAGAN'S ABRUPT DISMISSAL AFTER EIGHT YEARS OF SERVICE TO GE CAUSED MANY TO WONDER IF POOR RATINGS ALONE WERE THE CAUSE.

WITH GOOD REASON: SEVEN MONTHS BEFORE REAGAN'S TERMINATION, HIS PART IN THE SAG BLANKET WAIVER FOR MCA HAD HIM TESTIFYING IN WASHINGTON, D.C.

THE FBI AND THE JUSTICE DEPARTMENT'S ANTITRUST DIVISION HAD LAUNCHED AN INVESTIGATION...

...AND ON FEBRUARY 5, THE DAY BEFORE HIS 51ST BIRTHDAY, REAGAN APPEARED BEFORE THE GRAND JURY.

WHEN QUESTIONED ABOUT DECISIONS THAT WERE CLEARLY AMONG THE MOST IMPORTANT OF HIS TENURE AS PRESIDENT OF THE SCREEN ACTORS GUILD, REAGAN WAS ALARMINGLY OBTUSE:

WHICH COMPANY WAS THE FIRST TO CAPITULATE WITH RESPECT TO REPAYMENT FOR RERUNS?

THERE YOU HAVE ME. I WOULDN'T KNOW WHERE WE CRACKED THAT, AND IF YOU TELL ME I'LL HAVE TO TAKE YOUR WORD FOR IT.

INDEED, REAGAN SEEMED TO REMEMBER ALMOST NOTHING REGARDING ANY OF THE GUILD ACTIVITIES HE WAS QUESTIONED ABOUT.

I DON'T WANT TO APPEAR AS THOUGH I AM TRYING DELIBERATELY TO BE VAGUE, BUT, AS I SAY, I WOULD LIKE YOU TO REALIZE IN MY HISTORY OF HOLDING AN OFFICE WITH THE GUILD, MY MEMORY IS LIKE A KALEIDOSCOPE OF MEETINGS, THAT I AM SURE IF I SAT DOWN WITH SOMEONE AND STARTED IN, I COULD THEN RECALL THE DETAILS...

BY THAT SUMMER, WHEN THE GRAND JURY HANDED DOWN INDICTMENTS TO MCA AND SAG FOR VIOLATION OF ANTITRUST LAWS, GE HAD ALREADY DECIDED NOT TO RENEW REAGAN'S CONTRACT AND TO CANCEL THE MCA-PRODUCED SHOW.

ASK NOT WHAT YOUR COUNTRY CAN DO FOR YOU...

WITH DEMOCRAT JOHN F. KENNEDY NOW PRESIDENT, GE SOUGHT TO DISTANCE ITSELF FROM BOTH REAGAN'S CONSERVATIVE POLITICS AND THE POSSIBLE MCA SCANDAL.

TWO MONTHS LATER, THE GOVERNMENT DISMISSED ALL CHARGES AGAINST MCA AND THE GUILD. AS PART OF THE OUT-OF-COURT SETTLEMENT THE RECORD OF THE CASE WAS SEALED.

REAGAN WAS NEVER CHARGED.

NO, MR. WASSERMAN-- THANK *YOU.*

IN THE FALL OF 1962 REAGAN OFFICIALLY SWITCHED FROM DEMOCRAT TO REPUBLICAN, AT LEAST IN PART DUE TO THE INSISTENCE OF MCA VICE PRESIDENT TAFT SCHREIBER.

SCHREIBER WAS PROBABLY FAMILIAR WITH THE MESSAGE OF "THE SPEECH," AS WELL AS ITS EFFECT ON AUDIENCES.

WHILE KENNEDY'S ELECTION MAY HAVE HELPED SPELL THE END OF REAGAN'S DAYS AS GE SPOKESMAN, IT ALSO HERALDED THE BEGINNIING OF THE TELEVISED POLITICAL ERA.

70 MILLION AMERICANS HAD TUNED IN TO SEE THE PALE AND SWEATY RICHARD NIXON DEBATE THE TRIM AND TASTEFULLY MADE-UP KENNEDY.

SCHREIBER BELIEVED THAT REAGAN, AS A REPUBLICAN AND AS A TELEVISION STAR, WAS A MAN WITH A POLITICAL FUTURE HE COULD NURTURE.

FOR SOME REPUBLICANS, PRESIDENT EISENHOWER'S EIGHT YEARS IN OFFICE HAD BEEN A GREAT DISAPPOINTMENT. HE HAD CHAMPIONED A MULTI-BILLION-DOLLAR EFFORT TO CREATE A NATIONAL INTERSTATE HIGHWAY SYSTEM.

HE HAD "REFUSED TO GET INTO THE GUTTER" WITH COMMUNIST-CRAZED SENATOR JOSEPH McCARTHY.

TAIL-GUNNER JOE

AND HE HAD AGREED TO SEND FEDERAL TROOPS TO LITTLE ROCK, ARKANSAS, TO UPHOLD THE SUPREME COURT'S BROWN V. BOARD OF EDUCATION DECISION THAT AFRICAN AMERICANS WERE ENTITLED TO ATTEND THE SAME SCHOOLS AS WHITES.

IKE

MANY BELIEVED THAT EASTERN ESTABLISHMENT REPUBLICANS HAD HIJACKED THE PARTY AND ELECTED AN ADMINISTRATION THAT EMBRACED NEW DEAL SOCIAL WELFARE PROGRAMS, INCREASED TAXES TO PAY FOR THEM, AND LET COMMUNISM MAKE INROADS IN THE WESTERN HEMISPHERE.

IT WAS UNDER PRESIDENT WILSON, OF COURSE, THAT THE FIRST HUGE PARTS OF THE MARXIST PROGRAM, SUCH AS THE PROGRESSIVE INCOME TAX, WERE INCORPORATED INTO THE AMERICAN SYSTEM.

DESPITE KENNEDY'S 1960 VICTORY, A NEW RIGHT WAS ON THE RISE. PERHAPS ITS MOST EXTREME VOICE WAS ROBERT WELCH'S JOHN BIRCH SOCIETY.

SLIGHTLY TO THE LEFT OF THE BIRCHERS WAS THE ANTICOMMUNIST, ANTI-SOCIAL WELFARE, ANTI-INTEGRATIONIST PLATFORM OF ARIZONA SENATOR BARRY GOLDWATER.

IN THIS ENVIRONMENT, MCA'S SCHREIBER AND OTHERS SAW REAGAN AS A CROWD-PLEASING ALTERNATIVE.

THE NOVEMBER 22, 1963, ASSASSINATION OF PRESIDENT KENNEDY ONLY ADDED TO THE NEED FOR A COMFORTING CANDIDATE.

IN THE 1964 CAMPAIGN, DEMOCRAT LYNDON JOHNSON, WHO HAD BECOME PRESIDENT FOLLOWING KENNEDY'S ASSASSINATION, WAS RUNNING AGAINST GOLDWATER.

DEMOCRATS CAPITALIZED ON GOLDWATER'S REPUTATION AS AN EXTREMIST, GOING AS FAR AS TO SUGGEST THAT A GOLDWATER PRESIDENCY WOULD LEAD TO NUCLEAR WAR.

CALIFORNIANS HENRY SALVATORI, AN OIL DEVELOPER, AND ROBERT HOLMES TUTTLE, A CAR DEALER, SHARED SCHREIBER'S SENSE OF REAGAN'S POLITICAL POTENTIAL. THEY HAD SEEN REAGAN DELIVER "THE SPEECH" AT A CALIFORNIA GOLDWATER FUND-RAISER THEY'D SPONSORED AND WERE BOTH IMPRESSED.

IT WAS GOLDWATER'S PHILOSOPHY, BUT DELIVERED WITH THE REASSURING CHARM OF AN EXPERIENCED ACTOR.

AS CHANCES FOR A GOLDWATER VICTORY EVAPORATED IN THE WEEKS BEFORE THE ELECTION, SALVATORI AND TUTTLE LATCHED ONTO REAGAN.

USING MONEY LEFT OVER FROM PREVIOUS CALIFORNIA FUND-RAISERS, NATIONAL TELEVISION TIME WAS BOOKED, AND ON OCTOBER 27, 1964, RONALD REAGAN DELIVERED "THE SPEECH," NOW TITLED "A TIME FOR CHOOSING," TO A NATIONAL AUDIENCE.

AS IT HAD DONE HUNDREDS OF TIMES FOR NEARLY A DECADE, REAGAN'S SPEECH ELECTRIFIED HIS AUDIENCE. ONLY NOW THAT AUDIENCE NUMBERED IN THE MILLIONS.

IT ISN'T SO MUCH THAT LIBERALS ARE IGNORAN IT'S JUST THAT THEY KNO SO MUCH THAT ISN'T SO...

...TODAY WE ARE TOLD WE MUST CHOOSE BETWEEN A LEFT AND RIGHT...I SUGGEST TO YOU THERE IS NO LEFT OR RIGHT, ONLY AN UP OR DOWN. UP TO THE MAXIMUM OF INDIVIDUAL FREEDOM CONSISTENT WITH LAW AND ORDER, OR DOWN TO THE ANT HEAP OF TOTALITARIANISM...

...YOU AND I HAVE A RENDEZVOUS WITH DESTINY. WE CAN PRESERVE FOR OUR CHILDREN THIS, THE LAST BEST HOPE OF MAN ON EARTH, OR WE CAN SENTENCE THEM TO TAKE THE FIRST STEP INTO A THOUSAND YEARS OF DARKNESS.

REAGAN BECAME A POLITICAL STAR OVERNIGHT.

BUT REAGAN'S PERFORMANCE COULD NOT TURN THE TIDE FOR GOLDWATER. THE REPUBLICANS WERE ROUTED, CARRYING ONLY SIX STATES.

AS LBJ'S SECOND TERM BEGAN, TUTTLE, SALVATORI, SCHREIBER, AND A HANDFUL OF OTHERS, DUBBED REAGAN'S "KITCHEN CABINET," STARTED PLOTTING REAGAN'S POLITICAL CAREER.

AT FIRST, REAGAN ACTED WARY OF THE GROUP'S GRAND PREDICTIONS OF HIS POLITICAL PROSPECTS: FIRST CALIFORNIA, THEN THE WHITE HOUSE.

TO SET HIM AT EASE, THEY LAUNCHED THE "FRIENDS OF RONALD REAGAN" TO "EXPLORE THE DEPTH OF FEELING AND THE POSSIBLE COMMITMENT" HE COULD EXPECT WERE HE TO RUN FOR OFFICE.

A MAILING FROM THE FRIENDS OF REAGAN, SENT OUT TO PROMINENT REPUBLICANS, YIELDED ALMOST $135,000 IN POLITICAL DONATIONS, ENOUGH TO CONVINCE REAGAN THAT A 1966 CALIFORNIA GUBERNATORIAL CAMPAIGN WOULD BE TIME WELL SPENT.

BUT REAGAN'S EARLY SUPPORTERS ALSO KNEW THAT WINNING A STATEWIDE ELECTION WOULD REQUIRE APPEALING TO A BROADER RANGE OF VOTERS.

ANXIOUS TO WIN BOTH MODERATE REPUBLICAN AND DEMOCRATIC SUPPORT, REAGAN AGREED TO TEMPER HIS RHETORIC.

BUT IT QUICKLY BECAME CLEAR THAT, DESPITE HIS EAGERNESS, REAGAN'S COMMAND OF FACTS WAS SOMEWHAT... UNDERWHELMING.

WOULD YOU BELIEVE 15.1% OF THE POPULATION OF CALIFORNIA IS ON WELFARE?

ACTUALLY, IT WAS 5.1%. OUTSIDE HELP WAS NEEDED.

THE BEHAVIOR SCIENCE CORPORATION OF RESEDA, CALIFORNIA (BASICO), RUN BY PSYCHOLOGISTS DR. KENNETH HOLDEN AND DR. STANLEY PLOG, HAD BEEN CREATED TO IMPROVE INTERPERSONAL RELATIONSHIPS IN CORPORATIONS AND SCHOOLS.

HANDLING A BUDDING POLITICIAN LIKE REAGAN WOULD PRESENT NEW CHALLENGES.

48

REAGAN'S LACK OF PREPAREDNESS SHOCKED THE BASICO STAFF. HIS KNOWLEDGE OF STATE ISSUES WAS CONTAINED IN RANDOM PILES OF NEWSPAPER AND MAGAZINE ARTICLES HE'D CLIPPED FOR LATER USE...

...IF HE COULD FIND THEM AGAIN.

REAGAN'S MESSAGE TO THE PUBLIC WOULD STRESS THE ALMOST UTOPIAN ADVANTAGES OF UNRESTRICTED PRIVATE ENTERPRISE.

CALLED "THE CREATIVE SOCIETY" TO CONTRAST JOHNSON'S "GREAT SOCIETY" OF SOCIAL WELFARE, REAGAN'S APPROACH WOULD ENCOURAGE BIG BUSINESS, NOT BIG GOVERNMENT.

THE PROSPERITY THAT WOULD FOLLOW UNBRIDLED CAPITALIST "CREATIVITY" WOULD BENEFIT EVERYONE. AS REAGAN SAID:

ALL WE HAVE TO DO IS WANT IT BADLY ENOUGH.

GREAT CREATIVE

BUT REAGAN'S INSISTENCE ON THE POWER OF DREAMS COULD NOT COMPENSATE FOR HIS DRAMATIC BUT INACCURATE STATEMENTS.

CALIFORNIA CITY STREETS HAVE MORE CRIMES OF VIOLENCE THAN NEW YORK, MASSACHUSETTS, AND PENNSYLVANIA COMBINED.

THE SOLUTION WAS A SYSTEM REAGAN WOULD USE FOR THE REST OF HIS CAREER.

BASICO ASSEMBLED EIGHT CATEGORIZED VOLUMES THAT CONTAINED THOUSANDS OF INDEX CARDS OF ESSENTIAL "TALKING POINTS."

AS LONG AS REAGAN KEPT TO THE CARDS' SCRIPTED CONTENTS AND DIDN'T VENTURE OFF INTO UNCHARTED, EXTEMPORANEOUS TERRITORY, EVERYTHING WOULD BE FINE.

THE CARDS NARROWED REAGAN'S POSITIONS, FACTS, AND ANECDOTES DOWN TO CATCHY SOUND BITES THAT AUDIENCES COULD EASILY UNDERSTAND.

AND BASICO CONSTANTLY REVIEWED THE CARDS TO KEEP THEM CURRENT, ENSURING THAT REAGAN HAD THE APPROPRIATE CARD TO RESPOND TO ANY GIVEN QUESTION.

WITH REAGAN'S WORDS UNDER STRICT SUPERVISION, BASICO MOVED ON TO THE EQUALLY CRUCIAL JOB OF MONITORING HIS MOODS.

THEY HAD SEEN REAGAN LOSE HIS COOL WITH A PRIMARY OPPONENT AT A MEETING WITH A BLACK REPUBLICAN GROUP..

I RESENT THE IMPLICATION THERE IS ANY BIGOTRY IN MY NATURE! DON'T ANYONE EVER IMPLY I LACK INTEGRITY!

TO MINIMIZE STRESS, BASICO ENCOURAGED REAGAN TO TAKE NAPS EVERY AFTERNOON AND BEFORE EVENING SPEAKING ENGAGEMENTS.

THESE HELPED REAGAN MAINTAIN THE SUNNY, WELL-RESTED DISPOSITION THAT THE PUBLIC ADORED.

REAGAN EASILY WON THE PRIMARY AND MOVED ON TO CHALLENGE DEMOCRATIC GOVERNOR EDMUND "PAT" BROWN, WHO HAD LITTLE RESPECT FOR THE "CITIZEN CANDIDATE" OPPOSING HIM.

I'M RUNNING AGAINST AN ACTOR, AND YOU KNOW WHO SHOT LINCOLN, DONTCHA?

BROWN BADLY MISJUDGED HIS COMPETITION.

STUDENTS AT THE UNIVERSITY OF CALIFORNIA AT BERKELEY WERE SPEAKING UP AGAINST SCHOOL POLICIES. REAGAN, BELIEVING COMMUNIST FORCES WERE BEHIND IT, TOOK A HARD LINE AGAINST THE STUDENTS.

I'M SICK OF THE SIT-INS, THE TEACH-INS, THE WALK-OUTS.

WHEN I AM ELECTED GOVERNOR I WILL ORGANIZE A *THROW-OUT!*

JUST WEEKS BEFORE THE ELECTION, A WHITE POLICE OFFICER SHOT AND KILLED A FLEEING BLACK TEENAGER IN SAN FRANCISCO.

BROWN CALLED OUT THE NATIONAL GUARD AND THREE DAYS OF RIOTING ENSUED, REMINDING VOTERS OF THE RIOTS THAT HAD TORN APART THE LARGELY BLACK WATTS SECTION OF L.A. THE YEAR BEFORE.

REAGAN WON THE ELECTION BY A MARGIN OF ALMOST A MILLION VOTES.

TEN DAYS LATER, HE HELD A MEETING WITH THE SENIOR FRIENDS OF REAGAN TO BEGIN PLANNING A RUN FOR THE PRESIDENCY IN 1968.

ON JANUARY 2, 1967, JUST AFTER MIDNIGHT, REAGAN WAS SWORN IN AS GOVERNOR OF CALIFORNIA.

THE CURIOUS HOUR FOR OATH-TAKING, IT HAS BEEN SAID, REFLECTED ASTROLOGICAL FORECASTS. OTHERS MAINTAINED IT WAS MEANT TO DRAMATIZE REAGAN'S DETERMINATION TO SAVE CALIFORNIA FROM ANOTHER MINUTE OF HIS PREDECESSOR'S MISRULE.

DAYS LATER, IN HIS INAUGURAL MESSAGE, REAGAN REITERATED HIS APPROACH TO DEALING WITH THE COMPLEX PROBLEMS OF HIS OFFICE.

WE ARE GOING TO SQUEEZE AND CUT AND TRIM UNTIL WE REDUCE THE COST OF GOVERNMENT. IT WON'T BE EASY, NOR WILL IT BE PLEASANT...

THE GOVERNOR PROPOSED PROPERTY TAX RELIEF AND WELFARE REFORM IN ORDER TO REDUCE STATE SPENDING.

HE ALSO HAD HARSH WORDS FOR THE PROTESTING BERKELEY UNIVERSITY STUDENTS, SAYING THAT IF THEY COULDN'T OBEY THE SCHOOL'S RULES, THEY SHOULD "GET THEIR EDUCATION ELSEWHERE."

FREE SPEECH for CAL. STUDENTS

FSM

FREE SPEECH

FREE SPEECH MOVEMENT

NOW ALL THAT REMAINED WAS FOR REAGAN TO PUT HIS PLANS INTO ACTION. BUT THIS WAS EASIER SAID THAN DONE. AS PRESS SECRETARY LYN NOFZIGER LATER PUT IT:

HIS CAMPAIGN WAS RUN BY HIRED PEOPLE WHO THEN WALKED AWAY AND LEFT IT.

THEREFORE, WHEN HE WAS ELECTED THE BIG QUESTION WAS "MY GOD-- WHAT DO WE DO NOW?"

A YOUNG RECRUIT NAMED THOMAS REED HAD THE JOB OF SELECTING QUALIFIED PEOPLE FOR REAGAN'S STAFF.

HE WAS TOLD TO AVOID "PROFESSIONAL POLITICIANS," FINDING INSTEAD "CITIZEN-POLITICIANS" LIKE REAGAN HIMSELF.

MORE PRECISELY, REAGAN WANTED TO STOCK HIS ADMINISTRATION WITH SUCCESSFUL BUSINESS LEADERS, CONVINCED THAT THEY WOULD LEAVE THEIR CORPORATE JOBS TO HELP HIM BUILD A BETTER CALIFORNIA.

REED'S FIRST CHOICES DECLINED HIS OFFER...

SORRY, NO.

HEY! HOW ABOUT ME?

...FORCING HIM TO HURRIEDLY AMASS A TEAM OF NOT-SO-SUCCESSFUL BUSINESSMEN BEFORE TURNING TO REAGAN'S POSSIBLE 1968 PRESIDENTIAL BID.

THE HASTE AND DIMINISHED EXPECTATIONS WITH WHICH JOBS WERE DOLED OUT LED TO PROBLEMS.

GOVERNOR REAGAN'S FIRST CHIEF OF STAFF, PHILIP M. BATTAGLIA, WAS SUSPECTED OF BEING HOMOSEXUAL AND OF HIRING HIS HOMOSEXUAL FRIENDS TO FILL A VARIETY OF POSTS.

REAGAN'S CONSERVATIVE BASE WOULD DOUBTLESS CONDEMN EVEN A WHISPER OF HOMOSEXUALITY IN HIS GOVERNMENT. WHEN HIS ADVISERS INFORMED HIM OF THE RUMORS, REAGAN COULD SAY ONLY:

MY GOD-- HAS GOVERNMENT FAILED?

BATTAGLIA RESIGNED IN AUGUST, AND THE NEXT MONTH DETAILS OF THE STORY WERE LEAKED BY NOFZIGER, WHO LATER CLAIMED HE BELIEVED NANCY HAD SUGGESTED HE DO SO.

WHY DOESN'T SOMEONE DO SOMETHING ABOUT PHIL?

THAT NOVEMBER SYNDICATED COLUMNIST DREW PEARSON WONDERED IN PRINT "WHETHER THE MAGIC CHARM OF GOVERNOR RONALD REAGAN CAN SURVIVE THE DISCOVERY THAT A HOMOSEXUAL RING HAS BEEN OPERATING IN HIS OFFICE."

REAGAN CALLED PEARSON "A LIAR" AND THREATENED HE "BETTER NOT SPIT ON THE SIDEWALK" IF HE EVER CAME TO CALIFORNIA.

THOUGH THE ACCUSATIONS AGAINST BATTAGLIA WERE NEVER CONFIRMED, THE SPECTER OF THE "HOMOSEXUAL SCANDAL" WOULD LINGER FOR YEARS TO COME.

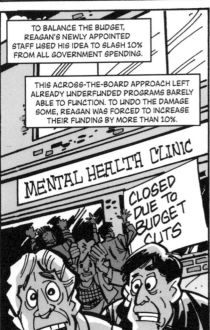

TO BALANCE THE BUDGET, REAGAN'S NEWLY APPOINTED STAFF USED HIS IDEA TO SLASH 10% FROM ALL GOVERNMENT SPENDING.

THIS ACROSS-THE-BOARD APPROACH LEFT ALREADY UNDERFUNDED PROGRAMS BARELY ABLE TO FUNCTION. TO UNDO THE DAMAGE SOME, REAGAN WAS FORCED TO INCREASE THEIR FUNDING BY MORE THAN 10%.

MENTAL HEALTH CLINIC

CLOSED DUE TO BUDGET CUTS

CUTBACKS ALONE WOULD NOT BALANCE THE BUDGET, WHICH NECESSITATED A 1967 TAX INCREASE. AFTER PROMISING TAX RELIEF, REAGAN HAD INSTEAD PASSED THE BIGGEST TAX HIKE IN THE NATION'S HISTORY.

CASHIER

REAGAN BLAMED CALIFORNIA'S FISCAL WOES ON HIS DEMOCRATIC PREDECESSORS, BUT CRITICS NOTICED THAT THE AMOUNT OF THE INCREASE ACTUALLY EXCEEDED THE AMOUNT THE STATE NEEDED TO PAY ITS BILLS.

WITH MONEY FILLING THE STATE'S COFFERS, THE MOST CHALLENGING PART OF REAGAN'S JOB AS GOVERNOR WAS ALREADY FINISHED.

HE WAS NOW FREE TO SPEND TIME TOURING THE COUNTRY, MAKING SPEECHES IN PURSUIT OF THE 1968 REPUBLICAN PRESIDENTIAL NOMINATION.

WHILE HIS EFFORTS FAILED TO SERIOUSLY CHALLENGE LIKELY NOMINEE RICHARD NIXON, AT LEAST REAGAN RETURNED HOME TO A NEWLY ROBUST CALIFORNIA.

THE SURPLUS LEFT A LASTING IMPRESSION ON THE PUBLIC. ACCORDING TO GARRY WILLS, REAGAN HAD "TURNED A SERIES OF BLUNDERS, COMPROMISES, AND BROKEN CAMPAIGN PROMISES INTO THE ILLUSION OF SHREWD CONTROL."

A PROMISE GOVERNOR REAGAN INTENDED TO KEEP, HOWEVER, WAS TO "CLEAN UP" THE STATE'S UNIVERSITY SYSTEM. REAGAN FOCUSED ON U.C. BERKELEY'S "LONG-HAIRED" FREE-SPEECH-ADVOCATING STUDENTS AND U.C. PRESIDENT CLARK KERR, WHOM REAGAN DEEMED THEIR PROTECTOR.

REAGAN KNEW THAT MANY CALIFORNIA VOTERS RESENTED BERKELEY'S EXCLUSIVITY; ONLY A HANDFUL OF THEIR CHILDREN WERE ADMITTED EACH YEAR. PUBLIC SENTIMENT WOULD BE BEHIND HIM THIS TIME.

WHEN HE CALLED THE PROTESTING STUDENTS "FILTHY SPEECH ADVOCATES" WHO SHOULD "OBEY THE RULES OR GET OUT," IT WAS EXACTLY WHAT ENVIOUS PARENTS WANTED TO HEAR.

WHEN IT WAS ANNOUNCED THAT THE UNIVERSITIES WOULD BEGIN CHARGING TUITION, KERR OBJECTED TO THE CALIFORNIA BOARD OF REGENTS. BUT REAGAN HAD ALREADY ALLIED HIMSELF WITH A MAJORITY OF THE MEMBERS-- AND KERR WAS REMOVED FROM OFFICE.

REAGAN SAID KERR'S OUSTER SAVED THE UNIVERSITY FROM HAVING TO ESTABLISH A COMMISSION TO "INVESTIGATE THE CHARGES OF COMMUNISM... ON THE BERKELEY CAMPUS. IT ALSO SAVED THE GOVERNOR FROM HAVING TO FIND OUT IF THOSE CHARGES WERE BASELESS.

RIDICULING STUDENTS BECAME A LYNCHPIN OF REAGAN'S OUT-OF-STATE, PRESIDENTIAL "EXPEDITIONARY" SPEAKING ENGAGEMENTS.

WE HAVE SOME HIPPIES IN CALIFORNIA. FOR THOSE OF YOU WHO DON'T KNOW WHAT A HIPPIE IS, HE'S A FELLOW WHO DRESSES LIKE TARZAN, HAS HAIR LIKE JANE, AND SMELLS LIKE CHEETAH.

AS STUDENT PROTESTS MOVED FROM FREE SPEECH TO THE WAR IN VIETNAM, BOTH UNREST AND REAGAN'S RESPONSE TO IT ESCALATED.

AFTER WEEKS OF VIOLENT PROTESTS AT BERKELEY, REAGAN DECLARED A STATE OF EMERGENCY AND CALLED ON THE CALIFORNIA HIGHWAY PATROL TO STOP THE "CRIMINAL ANARCHISTS" RESPONSIBLE.

ON MAY 15, 1969, POLICE FIRED INTO CROWDS OF STUDENTS, KILLING ONE AND WOUNDING OVER 50 PROTESTORS, AS WELL AS TWO REPORTERS.

AS EVENTS GREW EVEN MORE CHAOTIC, REAGAN CALLED IN THE NATIONAL GUARD AND DECLARED MARTIAL LAW ON THE CAMPUS FOR 17 DAYS.

BY 1970, REAGAN WAS MINCING NO WORDS:

IF IT TAKES A BLOODBATH, LET'S GET IT OVER WITH. NO MORE APPEASEMENT.

N HIS SECOND TERM, REAGAN SET HIS SIGHTS ON HIS LONG-STANDING DREAM OF CUTTING TAXES.

PROPOSITION ONE WAS A MASSIVE RESTRUCTURING OF THE CALIFORNIA TAX CODE. A STATEWIDE REFERENDUM WOULD BE NEEDED TO APPROVE IT.

YES on PROP ONE!

YES!

PROP ONE for the PEOPLE!

REAGAN HIMSELF HAD LITTLE NEED OF THE TAX REDUCTION BENEFITS OF PROP ONE.

THANKS TO SOME FANCY MONEY MANAGEMENT BY MCA, HE ALREADY PAID LITTLE IN STATE TAX (NONE AT ALL IN 1970).

$0.00

BUT THE DETAILS OF PROPOSITION ONE WERE CONFUSING-- PRACTICALLY INCOMPREHENSIBLE. REAGAN HIMSELF DEPARTED FROM HIS CUE CARDS TO CONCUR.

DO YOU THINK THE AVERAGE VOTER REALLY UNDERSTANDS THE LANGUAGE OF THE PROPOSITION?

NO-- HE SHOULDN'T TRY. I DON'T EITHER.

GIVEN THE GOVERNOR'S PERSONAL VOTE OF NO CONFIDENCE IN THE MEASURE, FEW WERE SURPRISED WHEN, IN 1973, PROPOSITION ONE WAS DEFEATED, 54-46%.

IT WAS SUPPOSED TO BE REAGAN'S CROWNING ACHIEVEMENT. INSTEAD, IT BECAME THE GREATEST DEFEAT OF HIS POLITICAL CAREER.

WITH PROPOSITION ONE DEFEATED, REAGAN AND HIS CLOSEST STAFF MEMBERS BEGAN SHIFTING THEIR ATTENTION FROM THE GOVERNOR'S OFFICE TO THE NATIONAL STAGE AGAIN.

IN 1973, DISTURBING EVENTS ON THAT STAGE LED REAGAN AND HIS ADVISORS TO CONCLUDE THAT A PRESIDENTIAL OPPORTUNITY MIGHT BE ON THE HORIZON.

WITH THE DISCOVERY OF THE ROBBERY OF DEMOCRATIC HEADQUARTERS AT WASHINGTON'S WATERGATE HOTEL, THE NIXON PRESIDENCY WAS UNRAVELING.

SENATE INVESTIGATIONS AND THE DISCOVERY OF SECRET PRESIDENTIAL TAPE RECORDINGS MADE DAILY HEADLINES. VICE PRESIDENT SPIRO AGNEW WAS FORCED TO RESIGN AMID CHARGES OF TAX EVASION.

RICHARD NIXON RESIGNED ON AUGUST 9, 1974, AND GERALD FORD, ALREADY ESTABLISHED AS VICE PRESIDENT, FOUND HIMSELF PROMOTED TO 38TH PRESIDENT OF THE UNITED STATES.

A REAGAN PRESIDENTIAL BID WOULD NOW MEAN CHALLENGING A SITTING REPUBLICAN PRESIDENT SEEKING REELECTION.

BUT WHEN FORD ANNOUNCED HE'D...

...GRANT A FULL, FREE, AND ABSOLUTE PARDON UNTO RICHARD NIXON FOR ALL OFFENSES AGAINST THE UNITED STATES...

...HIS POLL NUMBERS BEGAN TO SINK IN REACTION TO A PARDON THE PUBLIC FELT WAS UNDESERVED. REAGAN WAS BACK IN THE RUNNING..

...RIGHT UP TO THE REPUBLICAN NATIONAL CONVENTION, WHERE HE LOST THE NOMINATION TO FORD, WHO LATER LOST THE ELECTION TO DEMOCRATIC NOMINEE JIMMY CARTER.

REAGAN BELIEVED CARTER'S HEALING MESSAGE OF "INDIVIDUAL SACRIFICE FOR THE COMMON GOOD" WOULD NOT PLAY WELL WITH THE AMERICAN PUBLIC. HAVING LEFT THE GOVERNORSHIP IN 1975, REAGAN NOW SAW THE 1980 ELECTION AS HIS LAST TRY FOR THE PRESIDENCY.

BUT WHEN REAGAN ANNOUNCED HIS CANDIDACY ON NOVEMBER 13, 1979, MANY WONDERED IF AGE 69 WAS TOO OLD FOR THE JOB. IN AN INTERVIEW WITH TOM BROKAW, REAGAN'S CLAIM THAT HE WAS YOUNGER THAN MANY WORLD LEADERS ONLY INCREASED PUBLIC CONCERN:

GISCARD D'ESTAING OF FRANCE IS YOUNGER THAN YOU.

WHO?

GISCARD D'ESTAING OF FRANCE.

NBC

YES, POSSIBLY. NOT AN AWFUL LOT MORE.

PRESIDENT GISCARD D'ESTAING WAS, IN FACT, 15 YEARS YOUNGER. EITHER REAGAN DIDN'T KNOW WHO D'ESTAING WAS, OR HE WAS HARD OF HEARING.

ONCE IN THE WHITE HOUSE, HE WAS FITTED WITH HEARING AIDS.

BUT AS THE PRIMARY CAMPAIGN PROGRESSED, THERE SEEMED TO BE NO WAY TO DEFUSE THE AGE ISSUE.

REAGAN'S SUPPORTERS HAD AN IDEA. SINGLING OUT GEORGE H. W. BUSH AS THEIR LEADING OPPONENT, THEY ARRANGED A TWO-MAN DEBATE BEFORE THE NEW HAMPSHIRE REPUBLICAN PRIMARY TO PROVE WHO WAS THE BETTER CANDIDATE.

CAMPAIGN FINANCE LAWS MANDATED THAT ANY DEBATE NOT OPEN TO ALL CANDIDATES BE PRIVATELY FUNDED. ACCORDING TO THE REAGAN SIDE, THEY AND THE BUSH TEAM INITIALLY AGREED TO SHARE THE COSTS...

...BUT WHEN THE BUSH PEOPLE BACKED OUT, REAGAN, NOW THE SOLE SPONSOR, DECIDED TO OPEN THE DEBATE TO ALL CANDIDATES.

WHEN REAGAN ATTEMPTED TO EXPLAIN THE CHANGE OF PLAN, MODERATOR JON BREEN ORDERED THE MICROPHONES TURNED OFF. REAGAN EXPLODED (EVEN AS HE MISPRONOUNCED THE MODERATOR'S NAME):

I PAID FOR THIS MICROPHONE, MR. GREEN!!

RATHER THAN BEING VIEWED AS A GAFFE, REAGAN'S LINE, WHICH CURIOUSLY ECHOED THE 1948 SPENCER TRACY FILM *STATE OF THE UNION*...

DON'T YOU SHUT ME OFF! I'M PAYING FOR THIS BROADCAST!

...REMINDED VOTERS THAT REAGAN WAS STILL A "CITIZEN-POLITICIAN," WHICH DOUBTLESS HELPED HIM WIN THE NEW HAMPSHIRE PRIMARY.

AFTER NEW HAMPSHIRE THERE WAS NO LOOKING BACK. A MONTH BEFORE THE REPUBLICAN NATIONAL CONVENTION, GEORGE H. W. BUSH, THE LAST REMAINING OPPONENT, DROPPED OUT OF THE RACE, ONLY TO BE PICKED UP AS REAGAN'S RUNNING MATE.

NOW ALL THAT STOOD BETWEEN REAGAN AND THE WHITE HOUSE WAS PRESIDENT JIMMY CARTER.

THE CARTER PRESIDENCY WAS IN TROUBLE. INFLATION HAD REACHED 13%, UNEMPLOYMENT STOOD AT 8%, AND THE BUDGET DEFICIT HAD REACHED $60 BILLION.

CARTER'S BROTHER, BILLY, HAD ALSO BEEN CAUGHT ACCEPTING $220,000 FROM THE LIBYAN GOVERNMENT FOR LOBBYING ON THEIR BEHALF.

THEN, ON NOVEMBER 4, 1979, IRANIAN MILITANTS STORMED THE U.S. EMBASSY IN TEHRAN AND TOOK 52 AMERICANS HOSTAGE.

TWO ATTEMPTS TO RESCUE THEM HAD ALREADY FAILED. THE FIRST ENDED WHEN A RESCUE HELICOPTER CRASHED INTO A TRANSPORT PLANE, KILLING EIGHT U.S. SERVICEMEN.

BY THE TIME THE 1980 ELECTION WAS HELD, THE HOSTAGES HAD BEEN CAPTIVE FOR ALMOST A YEAR.

CARTER'S LAST CHANCE FOR VICTORY LAY IN CONVINCING VOTERS THAT A REAGAN PRESIDENCY WOULD BE WORSE THAN A SECOND CARTER TERM.

FIRST, CARTER'S CAMPAIGN SUGGESTED VOTERS COULD NOT TRUST THE VEHEMENTLY ANTICOMMUNIST REAGAN WITH THE POWER TO "PUSH THE BUTTON."

CAUCASIAN/ CHRISTIAN

AFRO-AMERICAN/ JEW

AND TO RAISE CARTER'S STANDING, THEY SUGGESTED THAT REAGAN'S POLICIES WERE RACIST AND WOULD SEPARATE THE NATION BY COLOR AND RELIGION.

CARTER WAS DESPERATE-- AND THE REAGAN TEAM KNEW IT. REAGAN HAD A COMMANDING LEAD WITH MALE VOTERS BUT STILL TRAILED WITH WOMEN.

EVEN REAGAN'S PROMISE TO APPOINT A WOMAN TO THE SUPREME COURT DID LITTLE TO CHANGE THIS.

REAGAN'S LONGTIME ADVISER STUART SPENCER SAID THAT, IN PRINT, HIS CONSERVATIVE RHETORIC FRIGHTENED WOMEN.

SEEING HIM SPEAK WOULD BE DIFFERENT. TO CINCH THE ELECTION, HE NEEDED TO DEBATE CARTER.

REAGAN REVEALS PLAN TO

THE DEBATE WAS HELD TEN DAYS BEFORE ELECTION DAY. WHEN ASKED ABOUT HIS "WARLIKE" TENDENCIES, REAGAN'S WARM RESPONSE USED THE WORD "PEACE" DOZENS OF TIMES.

THEN, WHEN CARTER MENTIONED REAGAN'S OPPOSITION TO MEDICARE, REAGAN SAW HIS OPENING. BEFORE REFUTING THE CRITICISM, REAGAN, IN HIS BEST HOMESPUN VOICE, SAID:

THERE YOU GO AGAIN.

IT WAS A PITCH-PERFECT DELIVERY, AS IF THIS WERE THE THOUSANDTH TIME HE'D ADMONISHED THE PRESIDENT FOR FIBBING.

IN THAT MOMENT, REAGAN CAPTURED THE HEARTS OF THE AUDIENCE AND, IT SEEMED LIKELY, THE PRESIDENCY OF THE UNITED STATES.

CONFIRMATION CAME ON ELECTION DAY 1980, WHEN REAGAN CAPTURED 51% OF THE VOTE TO CARTER'S 41%. EVEN THOUGH HE WAS NOW A "LAME DUCK" PRESIDENT, CARTER WORKED FEVERISHLY TO ACCOMPLISH ONE LAST TASK...

...THE RELEASE OF THE AMERICAN HOSTAGES IN IRAN.

AS CARTER NEGOTIATED, THE REAGAN TRANSITION TEAM, LED BY CAMPAIGN MANAGER WILLIAM CASEY AND FORMER CALIFORNIA STAFF MEMBERS EDWIN MEESE, WILLIAM CLARK, AND MICHAEL DEAVER, GOT TO WORK.

THEY PRIVATELY RAISED OVER $1.5 MILLION (BEYOND THE FEDERALLY FUNDED $2 MILLION) TO COVER TRANSITION COSTS, WHICH INCLUDED GENEROUS "RETAINERS" FOR THE MEMBERS OF THE TEAM.

AS HIS AIDES BEGAN THEIR TALENT SEARCH, REAGAN FAMILIARIZED HIMSELF WITH HIS NEW RESPONSIBILITIES BY MEETING WITH CARTER.

CARTER REMEMBERS BRIEFING REAGAN ON "15 OR 20 SUBJECTS" OF DOMESTIC AND FOREIGN POLICY, BUT WAS STRUCK BY THE FACT THAT REAGAN NEITHER TOOK NOTES NOR ASKED QUESTIONS.

REAGAN DID, HOWEVER, ASK CARTER FOR A COPY OF THE INDEX CARD HE'D BEEN REFERRING TO DURING THE MEETING.

LATER, HE WOULD USE HIS COPY TO REVIEW THE MEETING POINTS WITH HIS ADVISERS.

63

WITHIN WEEKS, REAGAN'S ADVISERS HAD PUT TOGETHER A CABINET MADE UP OF LONGTIME CALIFORNIAN ALLIES AND SOME LESS FAMILIAR FACES.

CASPAR WEINBERGER
SECRETARY OF DEFENSE

FINANCE DIRECTOR THROUGH REAGAN'S FIRST YEARS AS GOVERNOR. WOULD OVERSEE THE UNITED STATES' BIGGEST PEACETIME INCREASE IN MILITARY SPENDING.

WILLIAM FRENCH SMITH
ATTORNEY GENERAL

SMITH AND SUCCESSOR EDWIN MEESE PLACED CONSERVATIVE JUDGES IN COURTROOMS ACROSS THE COUNTRY—CONSIDERED REAGAN'S BIGGEST DOMESTIC SUCCESS

MICHAEL DEAVER
DEPUTY CHIEF OF STAFF

PUBLIC RELATIONS SPECIALIST FROM CALIFORNIA DAYS. IN CHARGE OF STAGING REAGAN'S APPEARANCES AND APPEASING THE FIRST LADY.

EDWIN MEESE
COUNSELOR TO THE PRESIDENT/ ATTORNEY GENERAL

LEADER OF NEW ADMINISTRATION'S SELECTION COMMITTEE. WAS GOVERNOR REAGAN'S CHIEF OF STAFF IN 1967. IN 1985 HE WOULD RISE TO ATTORNEY GENERAL.

JAMES A. BAKER III
CHIEF OF STAFF/ SECRETARY OF THE TREASURY

TEXAN CAMPAIGN MANAGER OF BUSH'S FAILED 1979 RUN AGAINST REAGAN. WOULD BECOME TREASURY SECRETARY IN 1985.

DONALD T. REGAN
SECRETARY OF THE TREASURY/ CHIEF OF STAFF

FORMER MARINE AND MERRILL LYNCH CEO. WHEN APPOINTED CHIEF OF STAFF IN 1985, RUN-INS WITH NANCY REAGAN HELPED LEAD TO HIS OUSTER.

WILLIAM J. CASEY
DIRECTOR OF CIA

WASHINGTON INSIDER AND DIRECTOR OF REAGAN'S SUCCESSFUL CAMPAIGN. CREDITED WITH ENSURING THAT THE IRAN HOSTAGE CRISIS WAS NOT RESOLVED UNTIL CARTER LEFT OFFICE.

ALEXANDER HAIG
SECRETARY OF STATE

ONLY CABINET MEMBER CHOSEN BY REAGAN HIMSELF. ENDORSED BY FORMER BOSS RICHARD NIXON.

REPLACED IN 1982 BY GEORGE P. SCHULTZ, FORMERLY PRESIDENT OF THE BECHTEL CORPORATION.

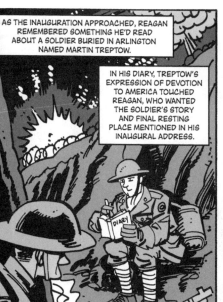

AS THE INAUGURATION APPROACHED, REAGAN REMEMBERED SOMETHING HE'D READ ABOUT A SOLDIER BURIED IN ARLINGTON NAMED MARTIN TREPTOW.

IN HIS DIARY, TREPTOW'S EXPRESSION OF DEVOTION TO AMERICA TOUCHED REAGAN, WHO WANTED THE SOLDIER'S STORY AND FINAL RESTING PLACE MENTIONED IN HIS INAUGURAL ADDRESS.

DIARY

BUT THE SPEECHWRITER, FINDING NO DIARY AND DISCOVERING THAT TREPTOW WAS BURIED IN HIS HOMETOWN IN WISCONSIN, REMOVED THE STORY FROM THE SPEECH. REAGAN DIDN'T APPROVE.

PUT IT BACK IN.

...

REAGAN'S JANUARY 20, 1981, INAUGURAL ADDRESS INCLUDED ALL THE FAMILIAR THEMES: REDUCING GOVERNMENT AND TAXES, EXPANDING THE MILITARY, DESTROYING COMMUNISM, AND INCREASING AMERICAN PRIDE.

IT ALSO INCLUDED THE STORY OF MARTIN TREPTOW, WHOSE BODY LAY ALONGSIDE THE OTHER MILITARY HEROES AT ARLINGTON CEMETERY.

ALTHOUGH THE PRESS SOON DISCOVERED TREPTOW'S TRUE FINAL RESTING PLACE, IT HARDLY MATTERED. FOR THE MOMENT, ALL OF AMERICA HAD BOUGHT INTO RONALD REAGAN'S DREAM OF AMERICA...

...ONE IN WHICH TIDY STORIES WON OUT OVER THE TRUTH.

WELCOME BACK TO FREEDOM

AS A CODA TO THE INAUGURATION, AT 12:33 P.M., DURING THE LAVISH INAUGURAL LUNCH, REAGAN WAS INFORMED THAT THE HOSTAGES HAD BEEN FREED AND HAD JUST LEFT IRANIAN AIRSPACE.

PLANNED OR PROVIDENTIAL, THEIR RELEASE GAVE THE CELEBRATIONS AN EVEN MORE FESTIVE AIR.

HOLLYWOOD TURNED OUT IN FORCE FOR ONE OF ITS OWN. NANCY'S WARDROBE, IT WAS SAID, COST $25,000.

THAT IT WAS THE END OF ONE ERA AND THE START OF ANOTHER...

...WAS APPARENT WHEN REAGAN INFORMED THE TELEVISION AUDIENCE THAT ALTHOUGH THE NATION WAS IN THE WORST ECONOMIC MESS SINCE THE DEPRESSION, ONCE HE CUT TAXES OVERALL BY 10% AND CURBED GOVERNMENT SPENDING, ALL WOULD BE WELL.

ALONG WITH CHARTS PROVING THE PLAN'S EFFICACY, REAGAN OFFERED UP THE HORRIBLE CONSEQUENCES OF INACTION:

1981 1982 1981 1982

WE CAN LEAVE OUR CHILDREN WITH AN UNREPAYABLE MASSIVE DEBT AND A SHATTERED ECONOMY, OR WE CAN LEAVE THEM LIBERTY IN A LAND WHERE EVERY INDIVIDUAL HAS THE OPPORTUNITY TO BE WHATEVER GOD INTENDED US TO BE.

THE BUDGET HE PRESENTED TO CONGRESS, ENTITLED "AMERICA'S NEW BEGINNING," WOULD COME TO BE KNOWN AS "REAGANOMICS." IT CONTAINED NO MENTION OF A BALANCED BUDGET.

THE BUDGET WAS TRUE TO CONVICTIONS REAGAN HAD HELD SINCE HE WAS IN HOLLYWOOD, BUT NOW THOSE CONVICTIONS WERE CALLED "SUPPLY-SIDE ECONOMICS."

SUPPLY-SIDERS BELIEVED THAT FREEING BUSINESSES FROM COMPLICATED TAXES AND REGULATIONS WOULD RESULT IN MORE MONEY FOR ALL.

I'VE GOT SO MUCH EXTRA MONEY NOW, I CAN SPREAD IT AROUND!

CHAMPIONING THE BUDGET WAS THE HEAD OF THE OFFICE OF MANAGEMENT AND BUDGET, DAVID STOCKMAN, AN AMBITIOUS YOUNG FORMER CONGRESSMAN FROM MICHIGAN WHO BOASTED TO REPORTERS THAT HE HAD NEVER TAKEN AN ECONOMICS COURSE.

SENATE MAJORITY LEADER HOWARD BAKER AND THE SENATE BUDGET COMMITTEE HOPED TO CURB THE DEFICIT BY SLOWING THE GROWTH OF SOCIAL SECURITY.

BUT THE PRESIDENT HAD PROMISED THE NATION THAT HE WOULD NOT TOUCH THE PROGRAM.

BESIDES, REAGAN BELIEVED STOCKMAN ALREADY HAD THE DEFICIT SITUATION UNDER CONTROL. STOCKMAN SAID THAT HE HAD IDENTIFIED $74 BILLION TO CUT FROM GOVERNMENT SPENDING AND PROMISED ANOTHER $44 BILLION IN WHAT HE CALLED "UNIDENTIFIED SAVINGS."

THE "UNIDENTIFIED SAVINGS," HE FAILED TO ADD, WOULD COME OUT OF THE POCKETS OF EARLY RETIREES IN A 10% CUT TO SOCIAL SECURITY.

BUT GROWING DISMAY WITH REAGANOMICS DIDN'T DIM THE PRESIDENT'S ON-RECORD OPTIMISM. NOR DID A WOULD-BE ASSASSIN.

ON MARCH 30, REAGAN WAS IN WASHINGTON, BEING ESCORTED TO HIS LIMOUSINE AFTER GIVING A SPEECH TO AN AFL-CIO GROUP. HE WAS WAVING TO THE CROWD WHEN—

WHAT THE HELL'S THAT?

TAKE OFF!

JERRY, YOU SONOFABITCH, GET OFF, I THINK YOU'VE BROKEN ONE OF MY RIBS.

uhn... I think...I've cut my mouth...

GO TO GW!!! GO TO GW!!!

THE EMERGENCY ROOM OF GEORGE WASHINGTON UNIVERSITY HOSPITAL WAS ONLY MINUTES AWAY.

DESPITE THE PAIN AND HIS DIFFICULTY BREATHING, WHEN THE CAR ARRIVED, REAGAN INSISTED ON MAKING A DIGNIFIED ENTRANCE.

EMERGENCY ROOM

I'LL WALK IN.

TWENTY FEET LATER, INSIDE THE EMERGENCY ROOM, HE COLLAPSED.

AS REAGAN LAY SEMICONSCIOUS, SURROUNDED BY A TEAM OF DOCTORS, THE STORY EMERGED.

JOHN HINCKLEY HAD BEEN STALKING THE PRESIDENT WITH INTENT TO KILL.

WAITING IN THE CROWD, HE FIRED SIX SHOTS, HITTING A POLICE OFFICER, A SECRET SERVICE AGENT, REAGAN'S PRESS SECRETARY JAMES BRADY, AND REAGAN.

DOCTORS SPOTTED A HALF-INCH SLIT UNDER REAGAN'S ARMPIT; THE BULLET HAD STOPPED ONE INCH BEHIND HIS HEART. AS HE DRIFTED IN AND OUT OF CONSCIOUSNESS A NURSE HELD HIS HAND.

Who's holding my hand? Who's holding my hand? Does Nancy know about us?

NANCY REAGAN, ALERTED DURING A WHITE HOUSE LUNCHEON, ARRIVED TEN MINUTES LATER.

Honey...I forgot to duck...

69

IN MOMENTS, THE DOCTORS HAD MADE THEIR DECISION TO REMOVE THE BULLET AND STOP THE BLEEDING. JUST BEFORE THE SURGERY WAS ABOUT TO BEGIN, REAGAN AWAKENED AGAIN.

I hope you're a Republican.

TODAY, MR. PRESIDENT, WE'RE ALL REPUBLICANS.

BACK AT THE WHITE HOUSE, TENSION WAS HIGH, AND SECRETARY OF STATE HAIG DIDN'T HELP MATTERS BY MAKING AN ALARMING ANNOUNCEMENT:

SO THEN THE HELM IS RIGHT HERE...FOR NOW, CONSTITUTIONALLY, UNTIL THE VICE PRESIDENT GETS HERE.

HAIG EITHER DIDN'T KNOW OR DIDN'T CARE THAT THE SECRETARY OF STATE WAS FOURTH IN THE LINE OF SUCCESSION.

SOON, HE BARGED INTO A TELEVISED PRESS BRIEFING, BREATHLESS AND VISIBLY SHAKEN, TO MAKE THE SAME CLAIMS.

AS OF NOW, I AM IN CONTROL HERE...

HIS UNHINGED, DISTINCTLY OUT-OF-CONTROL PERFORMANCE ON NATIONAL TELEVISION WAS UNFORGIVABLE. HIS DAYS IN THE ADMINISTRATION WERE NUMBERED.

AS THE PRESIDENT RECOVERED, NANCY WAS BESET WITH FEAR FOR HER HUSBAND'S SAFETY. SHE CONTACTED ASTROLOGER JOAN QUIGLEY.

I AM SCARED EVERY TIME HE LEAVES THE HOUSE... I CRINGE EVERY TIME WE STEP OUT OF A CAR OR LEAVE THE BUILDING.

FROM THEN ON, QUIGLEY WAS CONSULTED ON VIRTUALLY EVERY MOVE THE PRESIDENT MADE.

JAMES BAKER AND MICHAEL DEAVER HAD A DIFFERENT REACTION TO THE SHOOTING. SENSING A POSSIBLE PUBLIC RELATIONS BONANZA, THEY DECIDED TO PUT A BARELY RECOVERED REAGAN BEFORE A JOINT MEETING OF CONGRESS TO PUSH HIS BUDGET PACKAGE.

CAN REAGAN RECOVER? HOPE IS SHORT

THANKS TO SOME VERY FINE PEOPLE, MY HEALTH IS MUCH IMPROVED. I'D LIKE TO BE ABLE TO SAY THAT WITH REGARD TO THE HEALTH OF THE ECONOMY.

HAILED AS A HERO, WITH APPROVAL RATINGS TO MATCH, REAGAN WOULD CONVERT PUBLIC SENTIMENT INTO A MANDATE FOR HIS ECONOMIC PLAN.

UNDER THE CIRCUMSTANCES, CONGRESS HAD LITTLE CHOICE BUT TO PUSH THE PRESIDENT'S PLAN THROUGH.

THE TAX BILL WOULD REDUCE INCOME TAX BY 25% OVER THREE YEARS. THE DEFENSE BILL WOULD INCREASE MILITARY SPENDING BY $26.4 BILLION. AND A BIPARTISAN BUDGET BILL WOULD REDUCE GOVERNMENT SPENDING (THOUGH NOT NEARLY ENOUGH).

BY THE END OF JULY, THE BUDGET AND TAX-CUT PORTIONS OF REAGANOMICS HAD BECOME LAW, SETTING THE STAGE FOR THE REAGAN ADMINISTRATION'S "NEW BEGINNING."

BUT THE COUNTRY WAS ALREADY HEADING INTO A RECESSION. AS THE MONTHS WORE ON AND THE DEPTH OF THE RECESSION BECAME CLEAR, REAGAN'S RATINGS WENT INTO REVERSE.

NOMINATING A WOMAN, SANDRA DAY O'CONNOR, TO THE SUPREME COURT AS HE'D PROMISED, STAUNCHED HIS DECLINING POLL NUMBERS-- BUT ONLY TEMPORARILY.

IN OCTOBER, REAGAN ADMITTED THE COUNTRY WAS IN "A SLIGHT" RECESSION. DAYS LATER, HE SAID THE NOTION OF A BALANCED BUDGET BY 1984 WAS "NOT PROBABLE."

IN NOVEMBER UNEMPLOYMENT REACHED A SIX-YEAR HIGH.

THEN CAME THE VOTE OF NO CONFIDENCE IN REAGANOMICS FROM ITS AUTHOR:

THE WHOLE THING IS PREMISED ON FAITH... NONE OF US REALLY UNDERSTANDS WHAT'S GOING ON WITH ALL THESE NUMBERS.

IN THE *ATLANTIC* MAGAZINE ARTICLE "THE EDUCATION OF DAVID STOCKMAN," STOCKMAN SAID THAT SUPPLY-SIDE ECONOMICS WAS AN EFFORT TO REDUCE TAXES FOR THE RICH. HE'D COOKED THE NUMBERS TO MAKE THEM LOOK ROSY FOR THE REST OF THE COUNTRY.

WHILE POWERFUL REPUBLICANS DEMANDED STOCKMAN'S RESIGNATION, REAGAN, IMPERVIOUS TO CRITICISM, ASKED STOCKMAN TO LUNCH.

HIS QUOTES HAD BEEN TAKEN OUT OF CONTEXT, REAGAN SAID KNOWINGLY...

...YOU'RE A VICTIM OF SABOTAGE BY THE PRESS.

BUT REAGAN FOUND OTHER MEDIA REPORTS MORE COMPELLING.

IN DECEMBER 1981, MARTIAL LAW WAS DECLARED IN SOVIET-CONTROLLED POLAND IN THE HOPES OF CRUSHING THE FLEDGLING SOLIDARITY DEMOCRATIC LABOR MOVEMENT.

SoLiDARNoŚĆ

IN JUNE 1982, AS THE ECONOMY CONTINUED ITS DOWNSLIDE, REAGAN JOURNEYED TO VATICAN CITY TO MEET WITH POPE JOHN PAUL II, FORMERLY THE ARCHBISHOP OF KRAKOW, POLAND.

ALTHOUGH AT TIMES DURING THEIR MEETINGS REAGAN HAD TROUBLE STAYING AWAKE, POPE AND PRESIDENT AGREED TO SUPPORT EACH OTHER IN RIDDING THE WORLD OF THE COMMUNIST THREAT.

THE NEXT DAY, JUNE 8, REAGAN WAS IN ENGLAND EXPLAINING TO PARLIAMENT HOW THE U.S.S.R. WAS SOWING THE SEEDS OF ITS OWN DEMISE...

OVERCENTRALIZED, WITH LITTLE OR NO INCENTIVES, YEAR AFTER YEAR THE SOVIET SYSTEM POURS ITS BEST RESOURCES INTO THE MAKING OF INSTRUMENTS OF DESTRUCTION.

ALTHOUGH IT WOULD SEEM PROPHETIC IN RETROSPECT, AT THE TIME REAGAN'S SPEECH HAD EERIE ECHOES AT HOME.

TO EASE THE BUDGET DEFICIT BEING FUELED BY THE ONE-TWO PUNCH OF TAX CUTS AND U.S. MILITARY BUILDUP, REAGAN WOULD NEED TO TAKE ACTION. HE REVERSED ONE-THIRD OF THE PREVIOUS YEAR'S TAX CUTS, UNCONVINCINGLY CALLING IT TAX REFORM.

TO EVEN HAVE REFERRED TO THIS AS A TAX INCREASE, I THINK, WAS WRONG, BECAUSE IT WAS AN ADJUSTMENT OF THE TAX CUT THAT WAS PASSED LAST YEAR...

IN OCTOBER, ECONOMIC REPORTS WERE STILL DISMAL. THE NATIONAL UNEMPLOYMENT RATE WAS 10.1%. REAGAN'S APPROVAL RATING WAS JUST 42%.

WHEN, IN THE 1982 MIDTERM ELECTIONS, THE REPUBLICANS LOST CONTROL OF THE HOUSE AND REAGAN'S APPROVAL RATING DIPPED TO 35%, THE PRESIDENT QUIPPED:

I KNOW WHAT I CAN DO ABOUT THAT-- I'LL GO OUT AND GET SHOT AGAIN!

AS REAGAN'S VISION OF A VIBRANT AMERICA UNFETTERED BY TAXES SEEMED INCREASINGLY UNREALISTIC, HE ANNOUNCED AN INITIATIVE STRAIGHT OUT OF THE MOVIES:

SPECIFICALLY HIS MOVIE *MURDER IN THE AIR*, IN WHICH HE PLAYED BRASS BANCROFT, WHO HEROICALLY FIGHTS TO PROTECT A MACHINE CALLED THE INERTIA PROJECTOR THAT SHOOTS PLANES OUT OF THE SKY BEFORE THEY CAN BOMB THEIR TARGETS.

ON MARCH 23, 1983, BEFORE A NATIONAL AUDIENCE, REAGAN REVEALED WHAT WOULD BECOME KNOWN AS THE "STRATEGIC DEFENSE INITIATIVE."

WHAT IF FREE PEOPLE COULD LIVE SECURE IN THE KNOWLEDGE THAT...WE COULD INTERCEPT AND DESTROY STRATEGIC BALLISTIC MISSILES BEFORE THEY REACHED OUR OWN SOIL OR THAT OF OUR ALLIES?

INCREDULOUS, THE PRESS LIKENED THE PLAN TO *STAR WARS* AND THE PRESIDENT TO BUCK ROGERS. THEN REAGAN ADDED ANOTHER TWIST. ONCE THE DEVICE WAS COMPLETE...

...WE COULD OFFER TO GIVE THAT SAME DEFENSIVE WEAPON TO THE SOVIETS TO PROVE THAT THERE WAS NO LONGER ANY NEED FOR KEEPING THOSE MISSILES.

(WHICH WAS BOTH GENEROUS AND, SOME NOTED, A PLOT ELEMENT LIFTED FROM A 1951 FILM ENTITLED *THE DAY THE EARTH STOOD STILL*.)

YET EVEN AS REAGAN CLUNG TO VISIONS OF A SCI-FI SHIELD, HIS ADVISERS SAW THE VALUE OF THE PROPOSED SYSTEM AS A BARGAINING CHIP WITH THE SOVIETS.

EVENTS CLOSER TO PLANET EARTH WOULD SOON REDIRECT THE PRESIDENT'S ATTENTION TO MORE IMMEDIATE THREATS.

ON APRIL 18, 1983, THE U.S. EMBASSY IN BEIRUT, LEBANON, BECAME THE TARGET OF A TERRORIST SUICIDE BOMBING.

AMONG THE 63 PEOPLE KILLED WERE 17 AMERICANS. THE BOMBING WAS SEEN BY MANY AS AN ANGRY RESPONSE TO AMERICAN INTERVENTION IN A STEADILY WORSENING POLITICAL CLIMATE.

IN JUNE 1982, ISRAEL HAD INVADED LEBANON, THEIR ULTIMATE GOAL BEING A COORDINATED, MASSIVE BOMBING CAMPAIGN TO DESTROY THE PALESTINE LIBERATION ORGANIZATION, OR PLO.

HOWEVER, ISRAEL'S MILITARY HAD ALSO STOOD BY AS LEBANESE CHRISTIAN MILITIA GROUPS MASSACRED HUNDREDS OF MUSLIMS.

IN AUGUST 1982, AMERICAN MARINES ARRIVED TO TRANSPORT YASIR ARAFAT AND 10,000 PLO FIGHTERS TO SAFE HAVENS.

HOMMAGE AU COURAGE

BUT THE DETERIORATING SITUATION HAD KEPT THE MARINES IN BEIRUT. SEVEN MONTHS LATER THE BOMBER STRUCK.

THEN, ON SEPTEMBER 1, 1983, KOREAN AIRLINES FLIGHT 007 WAS SHOT DOWN BY SOVIET FIGHTERS AFTER WANDERING INTO SOVIET AIRSPACE. 269 PEOPLE WERE KILLED. AN OUTRAGED REAGAN CALLED IT...

...AN ACT OF BARBARISM, BORN OF A SOCIETY WHICH WANTONLY DISREGARDS INDIVIDUAL RIGHTS AND THE VALUE OF HUMAN LIFE...

BUT THE SPECTER OF COMMUNISM ALSO SEEMED TO BE RISING MUCH CLOSER TO HOME: IN THE TINY CARIBBEAN ISLAND NATION OF GRENADA.

REAGAN KNEW CUBA WAS ASSISTING GRENADA IN THE CONSTRUCTION OF A 10,000-FOOT AIRSTRIP. IF COMPLETED, HE BELIEVED THE AIRSTRIP WOULD BE USED TO TRANSPORT ARMS TO OTHER COMMUNIST-LEANING CENTRAL AMERICAN COUNTRIES.

ON OCTOBER 19, GOVERNMENT FORCES IN GRENADA EXECUTED PRIME MINISTER MAURICE BISHOP AND DECLARED A SHOOT-ON-SIGHT CURFEW. AMERICA, HOWEVER, DID NOT THEN LAUNCH AN INVASION.

RATHER, REAGAN INITIATED A "RESCUE MISSION" OF THE ALMOST 800 AMERICAN STUDENTS AT THE ISLAND'S ST. GEORGE'S UNIVERSITY SCHOOL OF MEDICINE.

THE FACT THAT THE COMMUNIST FACTION RESPONSIBLE FOR BISHOP'S MURDER AS WELL AS HUNDREDS OF CUBAN "ADVISERS" WERE CAPTURED IN THE PROCESS WAS AN ADDED BONUS.

30 HOURS LATER, WHEN THE EVACUATED STUDENTS ARRIVED IN CHARLESTON, SOUTH CAROLINA, AND KISSED THE TARMAC IN GRATITUDE, A POSITIVE PUBLIC RESPONSE TO THE MISSION WAS SECURED.

437 MA

BACK IN BEIRUT, ON OCTOBER 23, AT 6:22 A.M., A SECOND SUICIDE BOMBER STRUCK.

THIS TIME, THE TARGET WAS THE U.S. MARINE BARRACKS IN BEIRUT. 241 MARINES DIED IN THE BLAST.

THE NEWLY APPOINTED NATIONAL SECURITY ADVISER, ROBERT "BUD" McFARLANE, GAVE REAGAN THE NEWS AND REMEMBERED HIS REACTION AS "ONE OF DEEP GRIEF," FOLLOWED BY "A LONG, THOUGHTFUL STARING AT THE CARPET."

IN THE TELEVISED SPEECH THAT FOLLOWED, REAGAN LINKED ALL THE PREVIOUS MONTHS' EVENTS-- KAL 007, BEIRUT, AND GRENADA-- TO THE COMMUNISTS.

BUT AS VIVIDLY AS REAGAN WAS ABLE TO CONJURE A SOVIET-BASED "EVIL EMPIRE," IT WAS BECOMING HARDER AND HARDER TO CONNECT A FACE TO THE THREAT.

LONGTIME SOVIET PREMIER LEONID BREZHNEV HAD DIED IN NOVEMBER 1982 AND WAS REPLACED BY YURI ANDROPOV, WHO DIED NOT LONG THEREAFTER. ANDROPOV WAS SUCCEEDED BY KONSTANTIN CHERNENKO, WHO HIMSELF HAD ONLY A FEW YEARS TO LIVE. THE HARD-LINE SOVIET LEADERSHIP WAS DYING OFF; THEIR SUCCESSORS WOULD BRING NEW IDEAS.

DESPITE THE COSTS OF FIGHTING AN EVIL EMPIRE, IN HIS 1984 STATE OF THE UNION ADDRESS REAGAN ANNOUNCED THAT HE WOULD SOON BE LEADING AN ATTACK ON FEDERAL TAXES THAT RECALLED CALIFORNIA'S PROPOSITION ONE.

TREASURY SECRETARY REGAN WAS TO DELIVER A PLAN TO SIMPLIFY THE ENTIRE TAX CODE...

...IN DECEMBER, AFTER THE NOVEMBER PRESIDENTIAL ELECTION. THE TRANSPARENCY OF THIS DELAYING TACTIC WAS SO OBVIOUS THAT LAUGHTER FILLED THE ROOM, CAUSING REAGAN TO STOP MID-SPEECH AND WONDER ALOUD:

I SAID SOMETHING FUNNY?

THE PRESS SAW THE STATE OF THE UNION FOR WHAT IT WAS-- THE KICKOFF OF REAGAN'S REELECTION CAMPAIGN. WITH FOREIGN POLICY APPROVAL AT ONLY 38% AND THE 1985 BUDGET SUBMITTED THE NEXT MONTH ANTICIPATING A $180 BILLION DEFICIT, IT WAS A DUBIOUS BEGINNING.

BAD NEWS ALSO TRICKLED IN FROM LOS ANGELES, SAN FRANCISCO, AND NEW YORK, WHERE 3,700 AMERICANS, PRIMARILY YOUNG GAY MEN, HAD DIED OF A NEW DISEASE CALLED ACQUIRED IMMUNE DEFICIENCY SYNDROME (AIDS).

NOT UNTIL REAGAN MET WITH HIS OLD FRIEND, FELLOW ACTOR AND AIDS VICTIM ROCK HUDSON, WOULD THE DISEASE HAVE AN IMPACT ON HIM-- AND EVEN THEN, HE AVOIDED SPEAKING OF IT.

BUT REAGAN'S LONG-PROMISED ECONOMIC RECOVERY WAS FINALLY BEGINNING-- AS TAXES CAME DOWN, INTEREST RATES WERE FOLLOWING.

THE BIG PICTURE

TAXES

GROWTH

MOREOVER, REAGAN GOT POINTS FOR TAKING A BULLET, GETTING HIS BUDGET PASSED DESPITE THE CRITICS, AND STANDING UP TO STRIKING AIR TRAFFIC CONTROLLERS THAT SAME SUMMER...

... ALL WHILE CONJURING INSPIRATIONAL IMAGES OF A GLORIOUS AMERICA FOR THE TELEVISION AUDIENCE.

HIS DOZING OFF IN MEETINGS AND LOOSE GRASP OF THE FINE POINTS OF HIS PROGRAMS HAD LITTLE IMPACT ON THE MASS OF VOTERS.

MR. PRESIDENT? UH...MR. PRESIDENT?

REAGAN'S FEEL-GOOD REELECTION COMMERCIALS SOLD THE IDEA-- AND THE FEELING-- THAT HIS FIRST TERM HAD REAWAKENED A GREAT NATION.

ONLY REAGAN COULD UNDERMINE THEIR ROSY GLOW.

THAT SUMMER, WALTER MONDALE WON THE DEMOCRATIC PRESIDENTIAL NOMINATION.

LET'S TELL THE TRUTH. MR. REAGAN WILL RAISE TAXES, AND SO WILL I. HE WON'T TELL YOU. I JUST DID.

THE REPUBLICANS WERE DELIGHTED BY MONDALE'S CANDOR.

HOWEVER, REAGAN INADVERTENTLY ASSISTED MONDALE'S CAMPAIGN BY JOKING INTO A MICROPHONE HE BELIEVED WAS OFF.

MY FELLOW AMERICANS, I AM PLEASED TO TELL YOU TODAY THAT I'VE SIGNED LEGISLATION THAT WILL OUTLAW RUSSIA FOREVER. WE BEGIN BOMBING IN FIVE MINUTES.

ON AIR

WITHIN DAYS, MONDALE GAINED SEVEN POINTS IN THE POLLS.

AND IN THE FIRST DEBATE, A LESS SELF-ASSURED REAGAN TROTTED OUT "THERE YOU GO" AGAIN. ONCE FRESH, NOW STALE, THE ONE-LINER SUGGESTED HE WAS TOO OLD FOR THE JOB.

BUT BY THE SECOND DEBATE, REAGAN WAS BACK ON SCRIPT:

I WILL NOT MAKE AGE AN ISSUE IN THIS CAMPAIGN. I AM NOT GOING TO EXPLOIT FOR POLITICAL PURPOSES MY OPPONENT'S YOUTH AND INEXPERIENCE.

HE WON THE ELECTION IN A LANDSLIDE.

REAGAN WAS 73 AT THE START OF HIS SECOND TERM AND WAS ENJOYING A 62% APPROVAL RATING.

AFTER SHUFFLING HIS STAFF, REAGAN'S SECOND TERM WOULD APPEAR MORE PEACEFUL THAN THE FIRST. DONALD REGAN, NOW THE NEW CHIEF OF STAFF, WANTED TO "LET REAGAN BE REAGAN." BUT HE UNDERESTIMATED THE BEHIND-THE-SCENES WORK THAT WENT INTO THE PRESIDENT'S PUBLIC IMAGE.

THE FIRST SIGN OF TROUBLE CAME WHEN WEST GERMAN CHANCELLOR HELMUT KOHL INVITED REAGAN TO LAY A WREATH AT A GERMAN MILITARY CEMETERY.

REAGAN ACCEPTED. HOWEVER, NO AMERICAN TROOPS WERE BURIED IN GERMANY.

TRYING TO MAKE THE BEST OF THE SITUATION, DEAVER FOUND A PICTURESQUE CEMETERY IN THE TOWN OF BITBURG.

WHEN THE PRESS REPORTED THAT 49 NAZI STORM TROOPERS WERE BURIED THERE, A STUBBORN REAGAN REPLIED:

"THOSE YOUNG MEN ARE VICTIMS OF NAZISM ALSO... DRAFTED INTO SERVICE TO CARRY OUT THE HATEFUL WISHES OF THE NAZIS. THEY WERE VICTIMS, JUST AS SURELY AS THE VICTIMS IN THE CONCENTRATION CAMPS."

FEW AGREED WITH REAGAN'S RATIONALIZATIONS. WRITER AND HOLOCAUST SURVIVOR ELIE WIESEL, WHO WAS IN WASHINGTON TO RECEIVE THE CONGRESSIONAL GOLD MEDAL, ASKED REAGAN TO RECONSIDER.

MAY I...IMPLORE YOU TO DO SOMETHING ELSE... FIND ANOTHER WAY, ANOTHER SITE. THAT PLACE, MR. PRESIDENT, IS NOT YOUR PLACE. YOUR PLACE IS WITH THE VICTIMS OF THE SS.

BUT REAGAN HAD GIVEN HIS WORD TO KOHL, AND HE HEADED TO BITBURG IN MAY.

REAGAN'S RESOLVE PLAYED TO BETTER EFFECT WHEN ON JUNE 14, TWA FLIGHT 847 FROM ATHENS, WITH 153 ON BOARD, WAS HIJACKED BY A TERRORIST GROUP CALLING ITSELF ISLAMIC JIHAD.

FLYING FROM BEIRUT TO ALGIERS AND BACK AGAIN, THE HIJACKERS DEMANDED THE RELEASE OF HUNDREDS OF SHIITE PRISONERS TAKEN FROM LEBANON BY THE ISRAELIS.

REAGAN, KNOWING THE TV CAMERAS WERE ON HIM, MADE A SHOW OF NOT CANCELING A SINGLE MEETING.

THROUGH CLANDESTINE EFFORTS BY INFLUENTIAL IRANIANS, BY JUNE 30, MANY OF THE SHIITES WERE FREE ALONG WITH ALL THE HOSTAGES.

ALTHOUGH REAGAN SAID HE WOULD NOT NEGOTIATE WITH TERRORISTS, HE DID WRITE A THANK-YOU NOTE TO THE HEAD OF THE IRANIAN PARLIAMENT.

WHILE PUBLIC APPROVAL FOR REAGAN SOARED AFTER THE RETURN OF THE HOSTAGES, THE HIJACKING DREW ATTENTION TO SEVEN AMERICANS STILL HELD CAPTIVE IN LEBANON.

THE HOMECOMING WON'T BE COMPLETE UNTIL ALL HAVE COME HOME.

NATIONAL SECURITY ADVISER ROBERT McFARLANE HAD ONCE BEEN MORTIFIED WHEN REAGAN BLANKED ON HIS NAME. HE NOW SAW AN OPPORTUNITY TO BECOME UNFORGETTABLE.

McFARLANE MET WITH AN ISRAELI OFFICIAL TO DISCUSS IMPROVING RELATIONS BETWEEN AMERICA AND IRAN. INFLUENTIAL IRANIANS HAD ALREADY HELPED TO RESOLVE THE TWA CRISIS...

...AND WOULD BE WILLING TO DO MORE IN EXCHANGE FOR MUCH-NEEDED AMMUNITION AND REPLACEMENT PARTS FOR AMERICAN-MADE WEAPONS IN THE IRANIAN MILITARY.

McFARLANE KNEW THE SALE WOULD BE ILLEGAL; OPERATION STAUNCH FORBADE ARMS SALES TO IRAN IN THE HOPES OF FORCING A SETTLEMENT OF THE IRAN-IRAQ WAR.

BUT HE ALSO KNEW THE ISRAELIS WERE ALREADY SELLING ARMS TO IRAN.

McFARLANE LATER SAID HE TOLD REAGAN ABOUT THE PLAN AS THE PRESIDENT HEADED INTO THE HOSPITAL FOR COLON CANCER SURGERY.

HE HOPED IT WOULD LEAD TO THE RETURN OF THE SEVEN KIDNAP VICTIMS.

ON AUGUST 6, A DEAL WAS STRUCK: ISRAEL WOULD SELL THE ARMS TO IRAN, AND THE U.S. WOULD REPLACE THE SOLD ITEMS.

THE FIRST ORDER OF 96 ANTITANK TOW MISSILES WAS SHIPPED FROM TEL AVIV TO TEHRAN ON AUGUST 20. TEN DAYS LATER, ANOTHER 408 MISSILES WERE DELIVERED.

IN EXCHANGE, A SINGLE HOSTAGE WAS RETURNED. McFARLANE WAS CONCERNED BY THE FACT THAT THE OPERATION WAS BEING CONDUCTED BY ARMS DEALERS.

HE RECOMMENDED A HALT TO THE PROGRAM, BUT REAGAN INSTRUCTED HIM TO CONTINUE...

...OVER THE OBJECTIONS OF REGAN, SCHULTZ, AND WEINBERGER.

THERE ARE LEGAL PROBLEMS HERE, MR. PRESIDENT, IN ADDITION TO ALL THE POLICY PROBLEMS.

BUT REAGAN WOULD NOT HEAR OF IT. THE AMERICAN PEOPLE, HE SAID, WOULD NOT FORGIVE HIM IF HE LET DETAILS GET IN THE WAY OF FREEING THE HOSTAGES.

AND IF HE WENT TO JAIL FOR IT, HE SAID:

VISITING HOURS ARE THURSDAY.

IN DECEMBER OF 1985, NATIONAL SECURITY ADVISER BUD McFARLANE RESIGNED AND ASSISTANT JOHN POINDEXTER TOOK THE POST.

McFARLANE, HOWEVER, WAS NOT OUT OF THE PICTURE.

REAGAN SENT HIM TO LONDON TO MEET WITH AN IRANIAN ARMS DEALER TO NAIL DOWN AN ARMS-PER-HOSTAGE RATIO.

WHEN McFARLANE SAID THAT UNLESS LEGITIMATE IRANIAN POLITICIANS BEGAN PARTICIPATING IN THE PROCESS...

...WE HAVE NO INTEREST IN TRANSFERRING ARMS, AND CANNOT ENCOURAGE OTHERS TO DO SO...

...THE MERCHANT REPLIED:

84

MY CONTACTS ARE DESPERATE PEOPLE! THEY MUST FIRST GET STRONG AND TAKE POWER! THEN WE THINK ABOUT ALL THIS NICE POLITICAL SCIENCE!

GO POUND SAND!

McFARLANE HEADED BACK TO WASHINGTON WITH ANOTHER FAILURE TO REPORT.

McFARLANE AGAIN TOLD REAGAN THAT HE THOUGHT THE IRANIAN DEAL SHOULD BE ABANDONED.

COLONEL OLIVER NORTH, WHO HAD ALSO BEEN IN LONDON, DISAGREED, BUT KEPT HIS REASONS TO HIMSELF. HE INTENDED TO INFLATE THE PRICE OF THE WEAPONRY SOLD TO THE IRANIANS AND DIVERT THE PROFITS TO THE CONTRAS IN NICARAGUA.

AS CONGRESS HAD CUT FUNDS TO ANTI-MARXIST FORCES IN CENTRAL AMERICA, NORTH HAD TAKEN THE UNOFFICIAL "REAGAN DOCTRINE"...

..."WE MUST NOT BREAK FAITH WITH THOSE WHO ARE RISKING THEIR LIVES-- ON EVERY CONTINENT, FROM AFGHANISTAN TO NICARAGUA-- TO DEFY SOVIET-SUPPORTED AGGRESSION AND SECURE RIGHTS WHICH HAVE BEEN OURS FROM BIRTH"...

...AS HIS PERSONAL MARCHING ORDERS.

85

PROPELLED BY A NEW SENSE OF PURPOSE, THAT SPRING NORTH PRODUCED A FIVE-PAGE MEMO FOR McFARLANE'S SUCCESSOR, POINDEXTER, ENTITLED "RELEASE OF AMERICAN HOSTAGES IN BEIRUT."

USING SUSPICIOUSLY INEPT MATH, THE APRIL 4, 1986, DOCUMENT DETAILED THE PRICING AND PROFIT STRUCTURE OF ARMS SALES TO IRAN. AND UNDER A SECTION MARKED "DISCUSSION" IT PUT FORTH ANOTHER INITIATIVE:

$$\$ 17,000,000: \text{RETAIL PRICE TO IRAN}$$
$$- \$ 3,650,000: \text{OUR COST}$$
$$\$ 15,000,000 \; ???$$

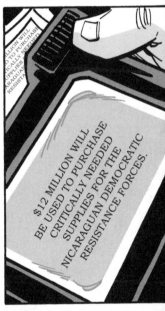

$12 MILLION WILL BE USED TO PURCHASE CRITICALLY NEEDED SUPPLIES FOR THE NICARAGUAN DEMOCRATIC RESISTANCE FORCES.

NORTH ADMIRED THE POETIC JUSTICE OF GETTING IRAN, AN AMERICAN ENEMY, TO FOOT THE BILL FOR THE OVERTHROW OF THE NICARAGUAN GOVERNMENT, ANOTHER AMERICAN ENEMY. IN HIS OWN WORDS, IT WAS...

NEAT.

IN HIS SECOND INAUGURAL ADDRESS, REAGAN HAD MADE A SURPRISE ANNOUNCEMENT THAT HE INTENDED TO HOLD A SUMMIT WITH HIS SOVIET COUNTERPART.

THE FOLLOWING NOVEMBER, THE PRESIDENT AND HIS WIFE FLEW TO GENEVA TO CONFRONT THE PERSONIFICATION OF HIS COMMUNIST NIGHTMARES.

BUT AS BRITISH PRIME MINISTER MARGARET THATCHER HAD PREDICTED, THE NEW SOVIET CHIEF, MIKHAIL GORBACHEV, AND REAGAN HIT IT OFF IMMEDIATELY.

A PLANNED 15-MINUTE DISCUSSION STRETCHED TO OVER AN HOUR.

WHERE THE TWO MEN AND THEIR COUNTRIES STOOD FARTHEST APART WAS PREDICTABLE: THE DEVELOPMENT OF THE SDI AND THE PROSPECT OF AN "ARMS RACE IN SPACE."

BUT SURPRISINGLY, THE TWO AGREED MORE THAN THEY DIFFERED, PRODUCING A PLEDGE TO REDUCE NUCLEAR ARMS BY 50%, AND A JOINT STATEMENT RESOLVING THAT "A NUCLEAR WAR CANNOT BE WON AND MUST NOT BE FOUGHT."

BY THE SUMMIT'S END, REAGAN WAS PREPARED TO MAKE A LEAP OF FAITH. WHEN CONSERVATIVE SPEECHWRITER PAT BUCHANAN PEPPERED REAGAN'S CLOSING REMARKS WITH ANTICOMMUNIST RHETORIC, REAGAN CROSSED IT OUT:

PAT, THIS HAS BEEN A GOOD MEETING. I THINK I CAN WORK WITH THIS GUY-- I CAN'T JUST KEEP POKING HIM IN THE EYE.

JANUARY 28, 1986. WITHOUT WARNING, TRAGEDY STRIKES.

73 SECONDS AFTER LIFTOFF, THE SPACE SHUTTLE *CHALLENGER* EXPLODES. AMONG ITS SEVEN-MEMBER CREW IS SCHOOLTEACHER CHRISTA McAULIFFE.

AND AMONG THE MILLIONS OF HORRIFIED WITNESSES WERE CHILDREN WATCHING IN SCHOOLROOMS ACROSS THE COUNTRY.

ON HEARING THE NEWS, REAGAN CANCELED THE STATE OF THE UNION ADDRESS SCHEDULED FOR THAT EVENING, AND INSTEAD READ A SHORT SPEECH THAT MASTERFULLY ACKNOWLEDGED THE NATION'S SORROW AND REACHED OUT TO THE YOUNGER VIEWERS:

I WANT TO SAY SOMETHING TO THE SCHOOLCHILDREN OF AMERICA WHO WERE WATCHING THE LIVE COVERAGE OF THE SHUTTLE'S TAKEOFF. I KNOW IT'S HARD TO UNDERSTAND, BUT SOMETIMES PAINFUL THINGS LIKE THIS HAPPEN.

IT'S ALL PART OF THE PROCESS OF EXPLORATION AND DISCOVERY. IT'S ALL PART OF TAKING A CHANCE AND EXPANDING MAN'S HORIZONS.

THE FUTURE DOESN'T BELONG TO THE FAINTHEARTED; IT BELONGS TO THE BRAVE. THE *CHALLENGER* CREW WAS PULLING US INTO THE FUTURE, AND WE'LL CONTINUE TO FOLLOW THEM.

MEANWHILE, CERTAIN NO ONE HAD FOLLOWED THEM, McFARLANE AND NORTH TOUCHED DOWN IN TEHRAN ON MAY 25, CARRYING IRISH PASSPORTS, SUICIDE PILLS, AND A CHOCOLATE LAYER CAKE FOR A FINAL ATTEMPT TO TRADE ARMS FOR HOSTAGES.

AFTER AN HOUR-LONG WAIT, THE IRANIAN REVOLUTIONARY GUARDS ARRIVED AND FOLLOWED McFARLANE AND NORTH TO A CARGO PLANE WHOSE HOLD WAS PACKED WITH MUCH-NEEDED SPARE MISSILE PARTS.

McFARLANE WAS INCENSED: FOR ALL HIS EFFORTS, THE IRANIAN GOVERNMENT HAD DONE NOTHING TO SECURE THE RELEASE OF THE HOSTAGES AND HAD SENT NO ONE WITH POLITICAL CREDENTIALS TO NEGOTIATE. HE'D HAD ENOUGH. FROM NOW ON, HIS STAFF WOULD HANDLE THIS JOB.

AND SO THE ARMS DEALERS WOULD WORK WITH NORTH, WHO PROCEEDED WITH THE SCHEME HE HAD OUTLINED TO POINDEXTER.

AS NORTH AND McFARLANE HEADED HOME, NORTH TRIED TO CHEER UP HIS COMPATRIOT BY FINALLY REVEALING THAT THE PROFITS OF THE ARMS SALES WERE GOING TO CENTRAL AMERICA.

AND THE PROFITS CONTINUED TO ROLL IN UNTIL OCTOBER, WHEN A CARGO PLANE WAS SHOT DOWN BY NICARAGUAN SANDINISTAS. ONE PASSENGER MANAGED TO PARACHUTE OUT, THREE OTHERS DIED.

THE WRECKAGE CONTAINED HUNDREDS OF AK-47S, AMMUNITION, AND RECORDS OF PREVIOUS SHIPMENTS OF WEAPONS DELIVERED TO THE CONTRAS. THE DEAD PILOT'S BUSINESS CARD IDENTIFIED HIM AS A MEMBER OF THE NATIONAL SECURITY COUNCIL.

THINGS GOT WORSE. THE LONE SURVIVOR, EUGENE HASENFUS, ADMITTED WORKING FOR THE CIA. HE SAID HE HAD RUN MORE THAN 50 SUPPLY FLIGHTS INTO CONTRA TERRITORY FOR THE OPERATION, WHICH ORIGINATED FROM THE WHITE HOUSE.

THEN ON NOVEMBER 3, 1986, THE STORY OF U.S. ARMS SALES TO IRAN SPILLED OUT ONTO THE PAGES OF *AL-SHIRAA*, A LEBANESE MAGAZINE.

THE IRANIAN GOVERNMENT QUICKLY CONFIRMED THE STORY.

ON NOVEMBER 13, REAGAN PRESENTED HIS CASE ON NATIONAL TV. HE DENIED THE CHARGE OF TRAFFICKING WITH TERRORISTS, INSISTING HIS ADMINISTRATION WAS ENGAGED IN A "SECRET DIPLOMATIC INITIATIVE TO IRAN."

REAGAN HAD AUTHORIZED ONLY A TRANSFER OF A SMALL NUMBER OF DEFENSIVE WEAPONS. HE FELT COMPELLED TO DESCRIBE IT:

...THESE MODEST DELIVERIES, TAKEN TOGETHER, COULD EASILY FIT INTO A SINGLE CARGO PLANE...

TO THAT LIE HE ADDED ANOTHER:

WE DID NOT-- REPEAT, DID NOT-- TRADE WEAPONS OR ANYTHING ELSE FOR HOSTAGES...

BUT ACCORDING TO THE NEXT DAY'S POLLS, 86% OF THE PUBLIC BELIEVED "WE" WERE DOING PRECISELY THAT, AND ONLY 17% APPROVED OF IT.

ON NOVEMBER 21, ATTORNEY GENERAL ED MEESE PROPOSED TO REAGAN THAT HE COLLECT THE FACTS ON THE IRAN SITUATION.

POINDEXTER LET NORTH KNOW HIS OFFICE WOULD SOON BE SCRUTINIZED.

NORTH'S RESPONSE WAS TO HEAD TO HIS OFFICE FOR WHAT HE CALLED A "SHREDDING PARTY" TO DESTROY STACKS OF POTENTIALLY INCRIMINATING DOCUMENTS.

WHEN NOT OPERATING THE SHREDDER, NORTH WAS REPLACING DESTROYED DOCUMENTS WITH SANITIZED "ORIGINALS."

CORRECTED ORIGINALS

NEVERTHELESS, WHEN MEESE'S INVESTIGATION PROCEEDED TO NORTH'S OFFICE, HIS STAFF FOUND A "SMOKING GUN"...

...A COPY OF THE MEMO FROM NORTH TO POINDEXTER DESCRIBING THE INFLATED PRICE OF WEAPONS TO IRAN-- AND THE DISBURSEMENT OF "RESIDUAL FUNDS" TO THE CONTRAS.

BY NOVEMBER 24, MEESE WAS READY TO TELL REAGAN THAT HE HAD UNCOVERED "A TERRIBLE MESS."

THE PRESIDENT MET WITH HIS ATTORNEY GENERAL AND CHIEF OF STAFF AT 4:22 P.M.-- LATE, FOR REAGAN-- TO HEAR THE DETAILS.

BOTH REGAN AND MEESE WOULD LATER SAY THEY FEARED REAGAN WOULD BE IMPEACHED.

THE FOLLOWING DAYS WERE A WHIRLWIND OF ACTIVITY. POINDEXTER RESIGNED; NORTH WAS FIRED; MEESE ANNOUNCED THAT MILLIONS FROM U.S. SALES OF ARMS TO IRAN HAD BEEN DIVERTED TO SWISS BANK ACCOUNTS FOR USE BY THE NICARAGUAN CONTRAS; REAGAN APPOINTED FORMER SENATOR JOHN TOWER TO HEAD A COMMISSION TO INVESTIGATE; AND REAGAN'S APPROVAL RATING DROPPED FROM 67% TO 46%.

CALLED BEFORE A COMMITTEE OF THE HOUSE, OLIVER NORTH, IN FULL MARINE UNIFORM, PLEADED THE FIFTH AMENDMENT AND REFUSED TO ANSWER QUESTIONS. POINDEXTER DID THE SAME.

CIA DIRECTOR CASEY COLLAPSED IN HIS OFFICE AND WAS RUSHED TO THE HOSPITAL THE DAY BEFORE HE WAS SCHEDULED TO SPEAK TO A SENATE INTELLIGENCE COMMITTEE.

WHEN REAGAN HIMSELF TESTIFIED IN FRONT OF THE TOWER COMMISSION, HE REPEATEDLY SAID HE HAD TROUBLE REMEMBERING DETAILS. BUT AFTER BEING ASKED FOR OVER AN HOUR IF HE'D AUTHORIZED ARMS SHIPMENTS TO IRAN, HE ANSWERED THAT HE HAD.

LATER, HE RECONSIDERED HIS TESTIMONY AND ASKED FOR A SECOND MEETING WITH THE COMMISSION. THIS TIME, HE READ HIS ANSWERS FROM A "TALKING POINTS" MEMO HE'D BROUGHT ALONG.

WHEN JOHN TOWER ASKED IF HE WAS AWARE OF A CERTAIN MISSILE SHIPMENT, REAGAN READ ALOUD:

"IF THE QUESTION COMES UP AT THE TOWER BOARD MEETING, YOU MIGHT WANT TO SAY THAT YOU WERE SURPRISED..."

PERHAPS SADDER THAN THE PRESIDENT'S PERFORMANCE WAS THE PLIGHT OF BUD McFARLANE.

McFARLANE'S TRUTHFUL TESTIMONY OF WHAT THE PRESIDENT KNEW AND WHEN HE KNEW IT WAS CONTRADICTED BY CHIEF OF STAFF REGAN, WHO MAINTAINED REAGAN HAD NEVER APPROVED THE ARMS SALES.

McFARLANE BELIEVED THAT REAGAN WOULD TELL THE TRUTH AND ACCEPT RESPONSIBILITY. IN McFARLANE'S MIND, THE PRESIDENT WAS THE ADMINISTRATION'S LAST HONEST MAN, A HERO AND A PATRIOT.

WHEN REAGAN CHOSE INSTEAD TO SKIRT ADMITTING ANY WRONGDOING, McFARLANE ATTEMPTED SUICIDE.

McFARLANE AWOKE IN A HOSPITAL ROOM, WHERE THE COMMISSION WOULD CONDUCT THEIR NEXT ROUND OF INTERVIEWS WITH HIM.

THIS TIME, HE WAS EVEN MORE PRECISE IN DESCRIBING WHAT THE PRESIDENT KNEW AND WHEN.

REAGAN RESPONDED WITH A LETTER TO THE COMMISSION:

I'M TRYING TO RECALL EVENTS THAT HAPPENED EIGHTEEN MONTHS AGO, I'M AFRAID THAT I LET MYSELF BE INFLUENCED BY OTHERS' RECOLLECTIONS, NOT MY OWN...THE ONLY HONEST ANSWER IS TO STATE THAT TRY AS I MIGHT, I CANNOT RECALL ANYTHING WHATSOEVER...

95

IN JUNE 1987, WHILE THE IRAN-CONTRA HEARINGS CONTINUED, REAGAN MADE A TOUR OF EUROPE.

SPEAKING BEFORE THE BRANDENBURG GATE THAT SEPARATED EAST AND WEST BERLIN, REAGAN GAVE AN ADDRESS THAT WOULD BE ENDLESSLY REPLAYED IN YEARS TO COME.

GENERAL SECRETARY GORBACHEV, IF YOU SEEK PEACE, IF YOU SEEK PROSPERITY FOR THE SOVIET UNION AND EASTERN EUROPE, IF YOU SEEK LIBERALIZATION: COME HERE TO THIS GATE! MR. GORBACHEV, OPEN THIS GATE! MR. GORBACHEV, TEAR DOWN THIS WALL!

ACHTUNG!

GORBACHEV WAS ALREADY SEEKING THOSE THINGS. HE WAS PUSHING FOR PERESTROIKA, THE RESTRUCTURING OF THE SOVIET ECONOMY-- AND GLASNOST, FREE DISCUSSION MEANT TO EXPOSE OLD-STYLE COMMUNIST POLITICIANS TO PUBLIC SCRUTINY.

HE AGREED TO MEET WITH REAGAN FOR A WASHINGTON SUMMIT.

THEIR PREVIOUS MEETING-- IN REYKJAVIK, ICELAND, ON OCTOBER 11, 1986-- HAD ENDED ABRUPTLY WHEN REAGAN, FURIOUS AT GORBACHEV'S INSISTENCE THAT THE STRATEGIC DEFENSE INITIATIVE BE CONFINED TO THE LABORATORY, STORMED OUT.

THE MEETING IS OVER. LET'S GO... WE'RE LEAVING.

BUT NOW, IN WASHINGTON, GORBACHEV DEMONSTRATED THAT HE HAD BEEN LEARNING WESTERN-STYLE POLITICS, HOSTING THE LIKES OF YOKO ONO, HENRY KISSINGER, AND BILLY GRAHAM FOR A CELEBRITY-STUDDED PARTY AT THE SOVIET EMBASSY...

...AND ENGAGING IN SEEMINGLY SPONTANEOUS PHOTO OPPORTUNITIES.

WHILE DRIVING DOWN CONNECTICUT AVENUE, ONE OF WASHINGTON, D.C.'S BUSIEST STREETS, GORBACHEV SHOUTED FOR HIS DRIVER TO STOP THE CAR-- THEN GOT OUT AND STARTED SHAKING HANDS WITH AWESTRUCK AMERICANS.

WHEN THE SERIOUS BUSINESS OF SIGNING AN ARMS REDUCTION TREATY CAME AROUND, REAGAN ANNOUNCED:

WE HAVE LISTENED TO THE WISDOM IN AN OLD RUSSIAN MAXIM... THE MAXIM IS: *DOVOREY NO PROVOREY*-- TRUST, BUT VERIFY.

GORBACHEV JUMPED IN WITH A QUIP:

YOU REPEAT THAT AT EVERY MEETING!

BUT REAGAN AGAIN THREATENED THE PROCESS WITH A DISASTROUS UNSCRIPTED AFTERNOON MEETING. AFTER GORBACHEV GAVE A GLOWING UPDATE ON PERESTROIKA, REAGAN BEGAN TELLING ANTI-SOVIET ANECDOTES.

...AND WHEN THE AMERICAN CAB DRIVER ASKED THE SOVIET SCHOLAR WHAT HE WAS GOING TO DO WITH HIS EDUCATION, THE YOUNG MAN SAID, "THEY HAVEN'T TOLD ME YET."

REAGAN, THE LEADER OF THE FREE WORLD, DID AS HE WAS TOLD THE NEXT DAY AND STUCK TO HIS CUE CARDS.

THE NEXT SUMMIT WOULD BE IN MOSCOW AT THE END OF MAY 1988.

REAGAN'S TEAM SPENT THREE MONTHS PREPARING THE SCRIPTS AND STAGING FOR THE VISIT.

AFTER GORBACHEV'S POPULAR PERFORMANCE IN THE STREETS OF WASHINGTON, D.C., REAGAN WAS ITCHING FOR A REMATCH:

WAIT UNTIL HE SEES WHAT I DO WITH HIS PEOPLE!

SPEAKING TO A CROWD OF CULTURAL FIGURES, REAGAN QUOTED A SOVIET FILMMAKER...

...BUT COULD HAVE BEEN SPEAKING ABOUT THE SECRET TO HIS OWN POLITICAL SUCCESS:

THE MOST IMPORTANT THING IS TO HAVE THE VISION. THE NEXT IS TO GRASP AND HOLD IT. YOU MUST SEE AND FEEL WHAT YOU ARE THINKING.

ON DECEMBER 8, 1988, MIKHAIL GORBACHEV CAME TO NEW YORK TO ADDRESS THE UNITED NATIONS. HIS UNEXPECTED ANNOUNCEMENT SHOCKED THE AUDIENCE:

TODAY I CAN REPORT TO YOU THAT THE SOVIET UNION HAS TAKEN A DECISION TO REDUCE ITS ARMED FORCES... BY 500,000 MEN.

THIS WILL BE DONE UNILATERALLY...

WITH HIS BUSINESS CONCLUDED, GORBACHEV MET WITH REAGAN AND PRESIDENT-ELECT GEORGE BUSH ON GOVERNOR'S ISLAND JUST OFF THE COAST OF MANHATTAN.

REAGAN WOULD BE PRESIDENT FOR JUST SIX MORE WEEKS; THIS WOULD BE A FINAL MEETING FOR THE TWO POLITICAL WARRIORS FROM OPPOSITE SIDES OF THE BATTLEFIELD WHO HAD SOMEHOW BECOME THE CLOSEST OF FRIENDS.

THOUGH REAGAN HAD ENVISIONED HIMSELF AND GORBACHEV REMOVING THE FIRST STONES FROM THE BERLIN WALL TOGETHER, WHAT HAPPENED IN THE FALL OF 1989 AFTER REAGAN HAD LEFT OFFICE WAS SUFFICIENTLY DRAMATIC.

AND AS THE BRANDENBURG GATE WAS OPENED ON DECEMBER 22, 1989, THE MEDIA SUGGESTED IT WAS REAGAN WHO HAD BROUGHT THE EVIL EMPIRE TO ITS KNEES.

AFTER TWO TERMS, REAGAN'S EFFORTS TO FULFILL HIS DREAMS OF AN AMERICA TRULY FREED FROM THE ENCROACHMENTS OF GOVERNMENT LEFT THEIR OWN LEGACIES.

THE VERY RICH WERE RICHER THAN EVER. THE AVERAGE ANNUAL PAY OF THE COUNTRY'S TOP BUSINESS EXECUTIVES ROSE FROM $3 MILLION IN 1980 TO OVER $12 MILLION IN 1988, DESPITE THE COLLAPSE OF THE STOCK MARKET IN 1987.

ALTHOUGH THE POOR HAD SEEN INCREASES IN INCOME, MORE CHILDREN WERE BEING BORN INTO POVERTY THAN EVER. AND THE SCOURGES OF AIDS AND CRACK HAD RUN UNCHECKED AS NANCY REAGAN URGED AMERICANS TO "JUST SAY NO" TO DRUGS.

THE DEREGULATION OF BUSINESS CHAMPIONED BY REAGAN AND PUSHED THROUGH BY LOBBYISTS HAD SET THE STAGE FOR A CRISIS IN THE SAVINGS AND LOAN INDUSTRY THAT WOULD COST PREDOMINANTLY MIDDLE CLASS TAXPAYERS $132 BILLION.

DESPITE REAGAN'S PROMISES OF CUTS IN THE SIZE OF THE FEDERAL GOVERNMENT, FEW WERE ACTUALLY MADE. THE BUILDUP OF THE MILITARY UNDER REAGAN AND HIS REFUSAL TO ASK AMERICANS TO SACRIFICE ANY OF THE SOCIAL SERVICES THEY HAD COME TO TAKE FOR GRANTED LED TO A BALLOONING DEFICIT.

YOUR FEDERAL DEFICIT-- A NEW WORLD RECORD!

HOWEVER, THE END OF THE COLD WAR HELPED REVERSE THE DEFICIT AFTER REAGAN LEFT OFFICE.

THE PHENOMENON OF THE "PEACE DIVIDEND" PLAYED A MAJOR ROLE IN PRESERVING THE REAGAN LEGACY OF ECONOMIC PROSPERITY.

BUT WHILE HIS ADMINISTRATION'S PERFORMANCE WAS DECIDEDLY MIXED...

...REAGAN'S PERFORMANCE AS AN ON-SCREEN POLITICIAN APPROACHED PERFECTION AS HE MADE HIS FINAL SPEECH FROM THE OVAL OFFICE:

MR. PRESIDENT-- WE'RE ON IN 5...4...3... 2...1--

ONE OF THE THINGS ABOUT THE PRESIDENCY IS THAT YOU'RE ALWAYS SOMEWHAT APART. YOU SPEND A LOT OF TIME GOING BY TOO FAST IN A CAR SOMEONE ELSE IS DRIVING, AND SEEING THE PEOPLE THROUGH TINTED GLASS-- THE PARENTS HOLDING UP A CHILD, AND THE WAVE YOU SAW TOO LATE AND COULDN'T RETURN. AND SO MANY TIMES I WANTED TO STOP AND REACH OUT FROM BEHIND THE GLASS, AND CONNECT. WELL, MAYBE I CAN DO A LITTLE OF THAT TONIGHT.

FURTHER READING

CANNON, LOU. *GOVERNOR REAGAN: HIS RISE TO POWER*. NEW YORK:
PUBLICAFFAIRS, 2003.

CANNON, LOU. *PRESIDENT REAGAN: THE ROLE OF A LIFETIME*. NEW YORK:
PUBLICAFFAIRS, 2000.

MORRIS, EDMUND. *DUTCH: A MEMOIR OF RONALD REAGAN*. NEW YORK:
RANDOM HOUSE, 1999.

REAGAN, RONALD. *AN AMERICAN LIFE: THE AUTOBIOGRAPHY*. NEW YORK:
POCKET BOOKS, 1999.

REAGAN, RONALD, WITH RICHARD G. HUBLER. *WHERE'S THE REST OF ME?*
NEW YORK: KARZ PUBS, 1981.

REEVES, RICHARD. *PRESIDENT REAGAN: THE TRIUMPH OF IMAGINATION*. NEW
YORK: SIMON & SCHUSTER, 2005.

SKINNER, KIRON K., ED. *REAGAN: A LIFE IN LETTERS*. NEW YORK: FREE
PRESS, 2003.

WILLS, GARRY. *REAGAN'S AMERICA: INNOCENTS AT HOME*. NEW YORK:
DOUBLEDAY, 1987.